"In an attempt to be edgy and culturally savvy, many in the church today have forgotten the ancient creeds that shaped the thinking of Christians for centuries. Winfield Bevins has provided us with a useful tool for rediscovering our historic foundations as Christians. I look forward to using this road map to guide new believers—young and old—on a journey of a lifetime."

—SCOTT THOMAS, president, Acts 29 Network;
author of *Theological Clarity and Application* and *Gospel Coach*

"I pastor a church that has tons of new believers. I always struggle to find theologically rich but life-practical resources to suggest to them. Winfield Bevins has done it! I highly recommend this book to those who want to know and grow in their faith."

—DARRIN PATRICK, pastor, The Journey, St. Louis, Missouri;
author; church planter

"*Creed* is a well-written book with the goal of helping Christians connect to the historic, orthodox faith. It accomplished that goal in a superb fashion. You will be edified and encouraged by this work on the Apostles' Creed, the Ten Commandments, and the Lord's Prayer. You will rejoice in the 'faith once delivered to the saints' that is embodied in these classics of Christianity."

—DR. DANIEL AKIN, president, Southeastern Baptist Theological
Seminary, Wake Forest, North Carolina

"We live in a culture marked by increasing biblical illiteracy in and out of the church. Winfield Bevins has taken timeless truth and shown how it can be used in disciple-making in a fresh and significant manner. I commend this book to you as a fantastic tool for church leaders to assist in the most basic of Christ's commands, His commission to make disciples."

—ALVIN L. REID, professor of evangelism and student ministry,
Southeastern Baptist Theological Seminary

"As I read through *Creed*, I continued to say to myself, *We need to use this book in our church*. Winfield Bevins has put together an eminently helpful guide to the basics of Christian faith. But there's more: *Creed* soaks each teaching in vintage Christianity through the use of historic vignettes and an accessible use of creeds. This approach connects twenty-first-century disciples to their vintage faith. Use it, especially for new disciples!"

—JONATHAN DODSON, lead pastor, Austin City Life

"Winfield says there is nothing new in his book. Good! That is exactly the point he wants us to get. What he correctly calls the 'historic tools of discipleship' have been with us and stood the test of time for good reasons. Of course they can just become words and ceremony, but if we follow Winfield's guidance and let them go deep into our souls as individuals and churches, they form the foundation on which to build a healthy spiritual life. This is a welcome refresher course from a pastor whose passion is the discipleship of God's people."

—STEPHEN SMALLMAN, instructor, CityNet Ministries of Philadelphia; author of *The Walk-Steps for New and Renewed Followers of Jesus*

"Winfield Bevins has written a book that helps readers of any level find out more about who God is, what He cares about, and the plans He has in store for His people. The connection between discovering the roots of Christianity and living a Christian life today makes this a great tool for helping people move from seeing God as a rule maker to seeing him as the Great Storyteller."

—MIKE ANDERSON, director, The Resurgence

"In a time of spiritual homelessness, *Creed* opens the door to the historic Christian faith. If you're tired of your own designer religion and open to something new but also old, tested, and enduring, *Creed* is the book for you."

—RAY ORTLUND, lead pastor, Immanuel Church, Nashville

CREED

CONNECT TO THE BASIC ESSENTIALS
OF HISTORIC CHRISTIAN FAITH

WINFIELD
BEVINS

NAVPRESS
Discipleship Inside Out™

Discipleship Inside Out™

NavPress is the publishing ministry of The Navigators, an international Christian organization and leader in personal spiritual development. NavPress is committed to helping people grow spiritually and enjoy lives of meaning and hope through personal and group resources that are biblically rooted, culturally relevant, and highly practical.

**For a free catalog go to www.NavPress.com
or call 1.800.366.7788 in the United States or 1.800.839.4769 in Canada.**

ISBN-13: 978-1-61747-147-6

Cover design by studiogearbox
Cover image by Jupiter Images

Some of the anecdotal illustrations in this book are true to life and are included with the permission of the persons involved. All other illustrations are composites of real situations, and any resemblance to people living or dead is coincidental.

Unless otherwise identified, all Scripture quotations in this publication are taken from The Holy Bible, English Standard Version (ESV), copyright © 2001 by Crossway Bibles, a division of Good News Publishers. Used by permission. All rights reserved. Other versions used include: the *Holy Bible, New International Version*® (NIV®), copyright © 1973, 1978, 1984 by International Bible Society, used by permission of Zondervan, all rights reserved worldwide; the New King James Version (NKJV). Copyright © 1982 by Thomas Nelson, Inc. Used by permission. All rights reserved; the New American Standard Bible® (NASB), copyright © 1960, 1962, 1963, 1968, 1971, 1972, 1973, 1975, 1977, 1995 by The Lockman Foundation. Used by permission; and the King James Version.

Library of Congress Cataloging-in-Publication Data

Bevins, Winfield H.
  Creed : connect to the basic essentials of the historic Christian faith / Winfield Bevins.
      p. cm.
Includes bibliographical references (p.   ).
ISBN 978-1-61747-147-6
1. Apostles' Creed. 2. Ten commandments. 3. Lord's Prayer. I. Title.
  BT993.3.B48 2011
  230—dc22
                                    2011009273

Printed in the United States of America

1 2 3 4 5 6 7 8 / 16 15 14 13 12 11

CONTENTS

ACKNOWLEDGMENTS

BOOKS ARE NEVER written in isolation. They are often the direct result of the encouragement and assistance of others. This book would not have been possible without the combined effort of many different people who have helped along the way. I am grateful for all who have had a part in making this book what it has become.

First, I am grateful to my family for their encouragement, support, and flexibility throughout this process. My wife, Kay, and daughters, Elizabeth and Anna Belle, have sacrificed precious time with their husband/father to make this writing project possible.

I am grateful to my spiritual family at Church of the Outer Banks. This project could not have been possible without their love and support. This book started among you and in many ways was written for you. In particular, I would like to thank Lynn and Sam for all of their assistance over the past several years.

I would like to thank Mike Miller, Barry Sneed, and the rest of the staff at NavPress for being so helpful throughout the entire writing process. I would especially like to thank Mike Linder, who graciously guided me through the editorial process and made it a joy to write this book.

I would like to thank Liz Heaney for all of her editorial advice and for helping me make this a more accessible and readable book, which is not as easy as it sounds.

Finally, I would like to thank Trey Brunson; without him, this book would not be a reality.

MY JOURNEY THROUGH THE PAGES OF CHURCH HISTORY

Early Christian teaching is simple and uncluttered; it cuts through the complexities of culturized Christianity and allows what is primary and essential to surface.

ROBERT WEBBER

I AM NOT the typical guy that you might think would write a book like the one you have in your hands. I was not raised in a traditional church. Actually, you could say I was not even raised in any church. I only attended church for an occasional Easter or Christmas service. Usually this was kicking and screaming. I felt that church was a cold and boring place for people who looked like they were attending a funeral.

Today I am a Christian. In fact, I am one of those culturally relevant, tech-savvy, artistic-type Christians who is addicted to using the iPhone and drinking way too much coffee. I love rock bands like Coldplay, Switchfoot, and U2. I am also a surfer. I live at the beach and keep a surfboard strapped to the top of my car just in case there is a good wave. Yes, that means on occasion I use words such as *dude* and *gnarly.*

I am also the founding pastor of Church of the Outer Banks in North Carolina. At our church we play loud music, use stage lighting, and serve coffee. In 2005 we began meeting in a home with only five people. Within a short time, the church outgrew the home and eventually grew to several hundred people; the growth brought many new challenges and opportunities. Many of the new people who began coming had little to no church background, and knew nothing about Christianity. It was a bit messy at the beginning.

One of our biggest challenges was helping new believers quickly understand the basics of the faith. We soon discovered that discipleship is particularly essential for the health and survival of new Christians and a new church. Consequently, we began to focus on growing from the inside by developing disciples instead of just growing our church numerically from the outside.

What was I going to teach these new believers? Like most young pastors, I looked to the latest books, programs, and curricula to teach the essentials of the faith, but they either lacked substance or were so academic that no normal person could understand them. It was discouraging trying to find a discipleship tool that helped real people connect with real doctrine in a way that was simple, yet profound.

Then it happened. I stopped looking for the next big thing and began to look to the pages of church history for answers. As I read books, biographies, and devotionals, I kept coming across the Apostles' Creed, the Lord's Prayer, and the Ten Commandments. At first I did not understand their contemporary relevance because they seemed so ordinary and basic. However, many times it's the ordinary things in life that we overlook and take for granted. Think about the basic essentials that we need for everyday life. Imagine if you didn't have a roof over your head, eyes to see, hands to touch, or legs to stand on. How often do we overlook or underappreciate these things? We do something similar with the Apostles' Creed, the Lord's Prayer, and the Ten Commandments. Slowly, I began to see their relevance for today's believers. Let me tell you why.

ARE THEY RELEVANT?

You may be asking yourself, *What is the importance of the Apostles' Creed, the Lord's Prayer, and the Ten Commandments?* or *Aren't they outdated in the postmodern world?* A few years ago I would have said the same thing. However, my tune has changed as of late.

Christianity wasn't invented yesterday and the church is much larger than one denomination or nationality. These three standards—the Apostles' Creed, the Lord's Prayer, and the Ten Commandments—have been used as a sturdy foundation for discipleship and doctrine for nearly two thousand years. If they were essential for the early generation of believers, shouldn't they be important for us as well? Why should we reinvent the wheel?

I suspect we do because of our obsession with the new. We live in a culture of change where we value everything new. We tend to focus on the "now" or the "moment" at the expense of the "eternal." But just because something is new doesn't mean it is better. Likewise, just because something is old doesn't mean it is useless and outdated.

Many contemporary Christians have historical amnesia and are missing vital aspects of the faith that are necessary for spiritual growth and maturity. Our lack of historic awareness can be remedied by revisiting the roots of the faith that have nourished believers since the time of Christ. Christians, such as you and me, are beginning to rediscover that church history has much to teach us about discipleship.

These three standards provide a simple and clear outline of the essentials of the faith that are universal for all Christians, regardless of denomination or affiliation. Sadly, most Christians get sidetracked over secondary issues rather than focusing on essentials. This is what C. S. Lewis had in mind when he wrote *Mere Christianity*: "To explain and defend the belief that has been common to nearly all Christians at all times."[1] Similarly, G. K. Chesterton referred to the Apostles' Creed as "understood by everybody calling himself Christian until a very short time ago and the general historic conduct of those who held such a creed."[2]

The Christian faith has multiple dimensions. Each of these historic standards addresses important dimensions of the Christian life that are profoundly interrelated. The Apostles' Creed addresses the doctrinal foundation, the Ten Commandments address the ethical foundation, and the Lord's Prayer addresses the spiritual foundation. When the doctrinal, ethical, and spiritual dimensions are woven together, they offer us a balanced model for the Christian life. These three summarize the heart of Christianity and offer us a glimpse of the Christian faith as a whole.

Many people have a small view of God because they have never taken the time to study His marvelous ways. The more you know about God and His redemptive plan for the world, the more you will fall in love with Him. The more you know about God, the larger your vision of Him becomes and the deeper your love for Him grows. This has certainly been true for me. By helping me understand the grand themes and doctrines of my faith, these three historic standards have enriched my walk with Christ and given me a newfound appreciation and love for Jesus.

WHY I WROTE THIS BOOK

Before you read any further, I must confess that you will not find anything new in these pages. The Bible says, "There is nothing new under the sun" (Ecclesiastes 1:9), and there is nothing original about this book. Rather than offering something new, *Creed* is about rediscovering historic tools for discipleship that can help you grow in your faith by learning the essentials of the Christian faith.

This book grew out of the process of wrestling with the need to help new and existing believers learn the essentials of the Christian faith. It is the result of trial and error and countless hours of prayer and study. It is my humble attempt at sharing some of the insights and golden nuggets I have found along the way.

Creed is written as a pocket guide to help the contemporary Christian in the twenty-first century connect to the historic faith of the church by focusing on the essentials. Rather than discussing every doctrine of the Christian faith, I have taken broad strokes to help you grasp the primary doctrines of the Christian church in one small book. It is not exhaustive, nor is it meant to be; rather, it is a summary of the essentials of the faith. Outside of these, we follow the motto of Saint Augustine: "In essentials, unity; in matters of opinions, liberty; in all things, love."

Creed is an ideal discipleship tool for believers, both old and new. New believers will find answers to basic questions about the Christian faith while mature believers will find renewal by revisiting these foundations. The first six chapters focus on the Apostles' Creed and explore the vital doctrines of the Creed and their relevance for today. The final two chapters discuss the Ten Commandments and the Lord's Prayer. I have written one chapter for each of them, not because they are less important, but to bring them into balance with the other doctrines we will examine in earlier chapters. Some of the chapters contain highlighted notes on various topics and significant Christians related to the chapter. You'll also find questions at the end of each chapter that can be used for individual reflection or group discussion.

I invite you on a journey to rediscover the grand themes and doctrines of the Christian faith as revealed in these three historical standards. Come and see what millions of Christians throughout the history of the church have known, loved, lived, and died for. Taste and see these truths for yourself. My prayer is that this book will deepen your devotion to Christ by helping you learn the essentials of the Christian faith and their relevance for today. Let's begin the journey.

PART 1

THE APOSTLES' CREED

The Doctrinal Foundation of the Christian Faith

THE APOSTLES' CREED, the most ancient and universally received of the creeds, succinctly summarizes the basic Bible doctrines. It begins with these simple words: "I believe." The English word *creed* is derived from the Latin word *credo*, which also means "I believe." The earliest form of the Apostles' Creed appeared around the second century, and it seems to have assumed its final form in the eighth century. Even though there is no historical justification for this belief, the creed is traditionally attributed to the apostles.

The early church used the Apostles' Creed to teach and disciple new believers in the faith. When someone became a Christian, that person was expected to be baptized as a public sign of the believer's death to the world, and born to new life in Jesus Christ. Before new believers could be baptized, they had to undergo an extended period of instruction in Christian beliefs that included memorizing the Apostles' Creed.

The Apostles' Creed is not a substitute for reading the Bible; however, it complements and summarizes the Bible's major themes in a beautiful and timeless fashion. It will help you better understand the doctrines of the Bible and develop a closer walk with God. Here, then, is the Apostles' Creed:

I believe in God, the Father almighty,
creator of heaven and earth.

I believe in Jesus Christ, his only Son, our Lord,
who was conceived by the Holy Spirit
and born of the virgin Mary.
He suffered under Pontius Pilate,
was crucified, died, and was buried;
he descended to hell.[1]
The third day he rose again from the dead.
He ascended to heaven
and is seated at the right hand of God the Father almighty.
From there he will come to judge the living and the dead.

I believe in the Holy Spirit,
the holy catholic church,[2]
the communion of saints,
the forgiveness of sins,
the resurrection of the body,
and the life everlasting. Amen.[3]

I BELIEVE: Finding Faith in the Story

The Bible becomes even more beautiful the more one understands it.

J. W. VON GOETHE

I GREW UP being very skeptical of organized religion, especially Christianity. This changed when I became a believer at the age of nineteen and Jesus Christ radically changed my life. At the time I didn't know much about Christianity, but I knew I believed in Jesus. I soon realized that I didn't know much else about my faith.

Not that Jesus ever gets old. He is all you or I will ever need. It's still all about Jesus, it's always been about Jesus, and it'll always be about Jesus. But, eventually, we need to know more about the faith because it helps us understand more about Him.

Once we put our faith in Jesus, it's common to have a lot of questions. For instance: Does everyone go to heaven? Is there even a heaven or a hell? Is there more than one God? What about evolution and science? What is the Bible? Or, one of my personal favorites, Are aliens real? (Believe it or not, people really do ask me this!) The truth is, questions are a legitimate way for people to find faith. You and I ought to be able to answer tough questions for ourselves and for others as well. The apostle Peter says, "Always be ready to give a defense to everyone who asks you a reason for the hope that is in you" (1 Peter 3:15, NKJV).

Where do we find answers to our questions about the Christian faith? We find them in the Bible. Time and time again, I have gone to God's Word to find personal strength and encouragement for life's greatest challenges. Although the Bible isn't a question-and-answer book, it is the place where we learn about God's plan and purpose for our lives. The Bible offers us foundations of faith so that we can find answers to many of life's toughest questions.

Reading the Bible can be a little overwhelming at first because it is so absolutely massive and contains many different doctrines, characters, stories, and themes. The good news is we don't have to be systematic theologians to read and understand God's Word. Reading the Bible is more like a marathon than a sprint, so I recommend that you start small and finish big. It will take a lifetime to study the entire Bible, and even then, you and I will never know all there is to know about it.

THE BIBLE STORY

I recently watched a movie starring Denzel Washington called *The Book of Eli*. It is a futuristic flick about a man who has the last Bible on earth. The story revolves around Denzel's character, Eli, a nomad in a postapocalyptic world who is called to take the last remaining Bible to a safe location on the West Coast of the United States. His travels take him across the country and down bandit-infested roads. He risks his life so that the Bible doesn't fall into the hands of the wrong people. In the end, the Bible is placed on a shelf between the Torah and the Koran.

The movie raises the question, Is the Bible just one of many other religious books? Some people think so. According to one survey, nearly 50 percent of American Christian adults believe that the Bible, the Koran, and the Book of Mormon all contain the same spiritual truths.[1] Others simply believe that the Bible is an ancient book with little value and relevance today.

Many people today are obsessed with facts and statistics. If we don't know what something is, all we have to do is go online and Google it or read about it on Wikipedia. We want information at our fingertips without having to do any reading to get it.

The Bible is not a newspaper or fact sheet. It was not the primary concern of the biblical writers to give us a set of statistics and details. Rather than focusing on every minute detail, they focused more on telling the story. They simply wanted to tell the Story of God.

So what is the Bible? It is best to understand it as the great Story. There is something about a good story, and all great stories echo the one great Story, the Story of God's redemptive plan for humankind throughout the ages. Children's author Sally Lloyd-Jones observes:

> The Bible isn't a book of rules, or a book of heroes. The Bible is most of all a Story. . . . You see, the best thing about this Story is—it's true. There are lots of stories in the Bible, but all the stories are telling the one Big Story. The Story of how God loves his children and comes to rescue them.[2]

Over half of the Bible is story or narrative that tells God is the great Storyteller, and the Bible is His grand Story of redemption. It is full of amazing tales about great men and women of faith whom God used to change the course of history and who influenced the world with the Word of God.

Story helps us understand the true nature of the Bible by focusing on the message and meaning rather than on just historical facts. Story relates truths through painting a picture, drawing the reader into its pages. While the Bible is historically significant, the authors were not primarily interested in recording history. They were more concerned about telling the Story of God's involvement in changing people's lives. Don't get me wrong; I believe the Bible is factual and true. But we cannot cram the Bible into our modern, historical, critical mind-set because it was written in an ancient Near Eastern world to inspire faith.

The Story is one grand narrative of God's redemptive love for lost humanity, and it is made up of three major events: Creation, the Fall, and redemption. These three events resonate in the imagination and have been depicted in art and song throughout history. The Story begins with Creation and climaxes with God's sending His Son, Jesus Christ, to die for our sins.

1. Creation. The Story begins with God. The Bible says, "In the beginning, God created . . ." (Genesis 1:1). Genesis tells how God created everything, including the sun, moon, stars, and the animals. Everything that God created was good. God also created man and woman in His own image to love one another and take care of the earth. God and humankind walked in unity and intimacy together.

2. The Fall. Then something terribly wrong happened. Adam and Eve disobeyed God and fell into sin by eating the forbidden fruit. They will forever be known as the guys who blew it. Their act of rebellion and disobedience is known as the original sin that brought a curse upon the earth. All humanity has tragically been affected by the Fall. Whether we realize it or not, we all share in the sin nature of Adam and desperately need the grace of God. The Bible says, "All have sinned and fall short of the glory of God" (Romans 3:23, NKJV).

3. Redemption. The Story doesn't end with the Fall. God became the hero of the Story and rescued and redeemed His people from their sin. The scarlet thread of the Bible is commonly called the *gospel*, which literally means "good news." The gospel is the underlying story of God's redemption that runs throughout the Bible and points to Jesus Christ as the Savior of the world. Jerry Bridges tells us the gospel is "not only the most important message in all of history, it is the only essential message in all of history."[3] The gospel is the key that unlocks the meaning of the Old and New Testaments. The great stories of the Bible testify to God's grace and love for His people. The gospel is the thread that helps you read through the Bible and apply it to your life.

THE STORYTELLER

Every story has a storyteller, and the Storyteller of the Bible is God, the Bible's author. The apostle Paul says, "All Scripture is given by inspiration of God, and is profitable for doctrine, for reproof, for correction, for instruction in righteousness" (2 Timothy 3:16, NKJV). God's Word was written by great men of faith who were directly influenced and inspired by the Holy Spirit. *Inspiration* literally means "God breathed." This means that the authors were vessels used by God to collectively write the greatest book ever written, the Holy Bible. God used these ordinary people to do an extraordinary thing—write the great Story.

The Lord still speaks through the great Story. I can remember the first time He spoke to me through His Word. I was a new Christian reading my Bible, but I had no idea what I was doing. One night, I was sitting on my bed, reading through the book of Psalms. When I read Psalm 51, the words on the page came to life and spoke to me about the very situation I was facing at that moment. The prayer of David became my prayer. The words of the psalmist in verse 10 (NKJV), "Create in me a clean heart, O God, and renew a steadfast spirit within me," touched me deep within, and I felt God begin to melt my cold heart. Since that night, I've continued the discipline of reading the Bible. I want to encourage you to begin to read God's Word for yourself and see how the Lord will speak to you from it.

SOMETHING OLD, SOMETHING NEW

The Bible is a collection of many different books with a unified theme. As a whole, it is a massive work made up of sixty-six books, divided into the Old Testament and New Testament, and spans thousands of years. Together, the books paint a picture of God's redemptive plan for the world. They are ancient documents that have been preserved over time and were eventually translated into our language. To give you a better grasp of the story these books tell, I want to share what they are, and where they came from.

The Old Testament

The Old Testament is made up of thirty-nine books, covering a two-thousand-year period beginning with the creation of the world, and closely recording the origins and history of the nation of Israel. It is old, and, I mean, very old. However, it's not called the Old Testament because it's old, but because that section reveals God's first covenant to humankind. A covenant is a special agreement between two parties that establishes a relationship based on mutual obligations and responsibilities. The Old Covenant refers to God's special relationship with the nation of Israel, which was based upon their obedience to God's law (see Genesis 17:1-19; Exodus 19–24).

The Old Testament includes history, poetry, and prophetic writings. It also contains some of the greatest stories ever told, such as the story of Moses and the Ten Commandments, Jonah in the belly of a whale, and Daniel in the lions' den—and let's not forget the story of Samson and Delilah.

The Old Testament was originally written in Hebrew for the Jewish people. During the time of Alexander the Great the Old Testament was translated into Greek by seventy-two Jewish scholars. The work was named the Septuagint, which means "seventy." It is usually abbreviated LXX, which is seventy in Roman numerals. By the time of Jesus, the Greek version of the Old Testament was widely used among Jewish communities everywhere because Greek was the predominant language of the Greco-Roman world. Early Christians also used this version of the Old Testament, including Jesus and Paul.

The New Testament

The New Testament is all about Jesus Christ and is considerably smaller than the Old Testament; it has twenty-seven books. If you've never read God's Word, the New Testament is the place to start. Begin by reading the Gospels—the first four books of the New Testament—which tell about the life, ministry, message, death, and resurrection of Jesus. Here you can find out more about Jesus' life and message for today. The Epistles are letters written to churches throughout the ancient Near Eastern world to address a variety of topics about the Christian life. The New Testament closes with the book of Revelation, which discusses futuristic events and the return of Christ.

The New Testament authors wrote down what Jesus said and did, sharing His teachings with others in the form of the Gospels. Early scribes made copies of the completed Gospels and other New Testament writings in many different languages, including Greek, Aramaic, and Egyptian. Most of these writings were written on papyrus, which was made from a reed plant. Other writers used parchment from the skin of animals. Eventually Christians began to use a more convenient book form known as the *codex*. This form contained stacked sheets of papyrus or parchment that were fastened together at one edge like a book. Basically, this was the earliest form of the modern book. These early copies were sent out to churches and Christians throughout the ancient Middle East.

The early church did not accept a book to be included in the Bible without significant evaluation and debate. Over time the early church began to recognize and endorse the authoritative books of the Bible out of necessity. Due to the spread of persecution and false writings, Christians had to decide which books they were willing to die for. The approved books were then called the canon of Scripture. *Canon* means "a straight rod" or "measuring stick." The formation of the Canon was an important step for the early church in distinguishing which writings were authoritative, and ensuring that future generations would know the true message of Jesus Christ.

Several points were used to determine and validate the canon of the Bible. First, a book had to be written by a prophet or an apostle, such as Mark, Luke, James, and Jude, or someone associated with them. Second, the book had to be in doctrinal agreement with the entire Bible and could not contradict or disagree with any previous

Scripture. Third, it had to already be accepted by the church as an inspired book.

PROFILES: Meet William Tyndale (1494–1536)

William Tyndale is called the father of the English Bible. He attended Oxford and Cambridge and eventually left the university world to translate the English Bible from the original Hebrew and Greek. Unfortunately, the church was opposed to his attempts at translating the Bible into the language of the English people and he was forced to go into hiding. He became known as "God's outlaw."

Despite persecution and attempts on his life, Tyndale eventually succeeded in translating the entire New Testament and some of the Old Testament into English. In 1535, he was betrayed by a friend and arrested. He paid for his work with his life and was strangled and burned at the stake near Brussels. However, in the end, Tyndale was victorious because his translation became the basis for English translations of the Bible since that time.

HOW IT CAME TO US

Most people don't have a clue as to how we got the modern Bible. I certainly didn't when I first became a Christian. While it's not necessary to understand the origins of the Bible to become a believer, it's important to understand how it all came together so that you can explain it to others. Many people today are skeptical about the Bible, especially when it comes to translations. Popular novels like *The Da Vinci Code* and *Holy Blood, Holy Grail* challenge the credibility of the Bible, and ultimately the Christian faith.

Here's an overview of how we got the modern Bible we read from today. As the Christian faith spread throughout the world, the need for translations increased. Over time the biblical documents were translated into other languages so that people from other nations could read the Bible for themselves. At first, these Bibles were translated by hand. It took up to three hundred working days to produce a single copy of the Bible. This means that it took one scribe roughly an entire year to produce a single copy of the Bible. This made the widespread distribution of the Bible virtually impossible.

Everything changed when a German goldsmith named Johannes Gutenberg invented the printing press. In August 1456, the first published Bible was printed from the press. Gutenberg's press opened the door for others to begin to translate the Bible into various languages.

Not everyone was happy about this advancement. Many translators, including William Tyndale, were persecuted for translating the Bible into the language of common people, yet they persevered because they wanted everyone to have the Bible in his or her own language. In the 1380s, John Wycliffe produced the first English translation of the New Testament from the Latin Vulgate. During 1525–1526, William Tyndale wrote a translation of the New Testament from the original Greek. In 1522, Martin Luther published the New Testament in German; in 1534, he published the Old Testament. Later, in 1611, King James commissioned the popular King James Version of the Bible in English, which is still used today by many churches.

I am thankful for the blood, sweat, and tears of faithful men like Martin Luther, William Tyndale, and John Wycliffe, who risked their lives so that we could have modern translations of the Bible. Our modern English translations of the Bible, such as the English Standard Version, New International Version, and New American Standard Version, have been given with a price, and we should have great respect for the heritage of Bible translators who made these possible.

GOING DEEPER: Reading Your Bible

Here are several suggestions for getting the most from studying your Bible.

1. Choose a good translation that is easy for you to read, such as the New International Version, the New American Standard Version, or *The Message*.
2. Study your Bible daily. There is no substitute for a regular and systematic study of Scripture. You will be surprised how much you gain from reading your Bible daily.
3. Find a time that works for you. Every one of us has a different rhythm or time of the day that is best for us to study the Bible. For example, my wife is a morning person and likes to read the Bible in the morning, while I am a night person and the evenings work best for me.
4. Take notes and underline in your Bible. This will help you remember what you have learned and help you go back and find important places you have marked in your Bible.
5. Allow yourself time to think about what the Bible is saying. People try to read the Bible like a novel, without allowing time to take it to heart. It doesn't have to be long; try to take twenty to thirty minutes to study each day.
6. Memorize Scripture. Make some note cards and memorize several Scriptures every week.
7. Share what you learn in the Bible with others. Teaching is one of the best ways to reinforce what you have learned.

REFLECT AND RESPOND

The fact that you are reading this book means you want to know more about God and His Word. Learning about the doctrines of the Bible can help you do just that, as well as help you better understand the Bible as a whole. The more we learn about God and His Word, the more we are able to know Him personally. A. W. Tozer reminds us, "The Bible is not an end in itself, but a means to bring men to an intimate and satisfying knowledge of God, that they may enter into Him, that they may delight in His Presence, may taste and know the inner sweetness of the very God Himself in the core and center of their hearts."[4]

Before you read any further, I recommend that you do a couple of things. Take some time to explore your Bible. If you don't have one already, go out and buy one. Begin to familiarize yourself with your Bible by reading the table of contents and flipping through the pages to see how God's Word is organized and put together. It is God's Story written for you, so take time to get to know it.

I would like you to reflect on the following thoughts. Think about how old the Bible actually is and how amazing it is that you and I have a Bible in our own language. What a great privilege and honor it is to actually own a Bible. Also, consider the men and women who gave their lives so that you and I could have a Bible in our own language.

As you begin to read the Bible every day, it will cause you to grow and mature spiritually. As you study, it will strengthen your faith, speak to your heart, and guide you in all of life's tough decisions. As you continue to read it, God will reveal His plans and purposes for your life. Take some time to seek and find out what He is telling you from His Word.

1. What are some of the different ideas that people have about the Bible? Why do you think there are so many different views? Where do you think these different ideas originated?
2. The Bible is the Story of God. What is the overarching theme of the Story and how do the individual stories make it unique?
3. Most people don't understand how we got the Bible. Do your best to recount the process of how we got the Bible. How does understanding that process make the Bible more credible?
4. Do you believe the Bible is still relevant? Why or why not? If you believe it is relevant, what are some ways you can apply the Bible to your everyday life?

CHAPTER 2

GOD: The Great Storyteller

I had always felt life first as a story: and if there is a story there is a story-teller.

G. K. CHESTERTON

"IN GOD WE trust," is a phrase that used to be as American as apple pie, but the spiritual landscape of the United States is rapidly changing. Today the big question isn't, "Do people believe in God?" It is, "Which God do they believe in?" There are hundreds of religions in North America alone.

The book of Judges tells us of a time in Israel's history when, "There arose another generation after them who did not know the LORD or the work that he had done for Israel" (2:10). In a similar way, there are a growing number of people in North America who are *radically unchurched*. Alvin Reid defines the radically unchurched as those "who have no clear personal understanding of the message of the gospel, and who have had little or no contact with a Bible-teaching, Christ-honoring church." They make up nearly 40 percent of the population.[1]

While most of these unchurched people wouldn't call themselves religious, they would consider themselves spiritual. Spirituality is in style, and business is booming. People haven't given up on faith; they are just looking for it outside the four walls of the traditional church.

Alternative religions such as Islam, Buddhism, Hinduism, and other religions are experiencing explosive gowth here, and around the world.

Many people in North America no longer have a biblical worldview. A worldview is the way in which we understand reality and perceive the world around us. To have a biblical worldview means that we see the world through the lenses of the Word of God.

Several weeks ago I had a conversation with a young man on the beach about God, Jesus, and Christianity in general. He proceeded to tell me that he believed all religions were essentially the same and should all come together as one. The shocking thing for me wasn't that he did not hold a biblical worldview, but that he was a deacon in his local Christian church. He is not alone. Most Americans do not have a biblical worldview. Sadly, this includes many people who call themselves Christians.

The Apostles' Creed stands in stark contrast to our postmodern society by radically calling us back to a biblical worldview. It begins with the declaration, "I believe in God, the Father almighty, creator of heaven and earth." Although short, this bold declaration is loaded with deep truths about God that reveal His nature, character, love, and redemptive plan for humankind. In this chapter, I want us to explore the uniqueness of the character of God and the proper response to Him in light of who He is.

WHO'S YOUR DADDY?

Some people see God as a transcendent deity who is disconnected from the real world and not involved in people's lives. Others think God is waiting around to strike them with a lightning bolt every time they do something wrong. The truth is God is our Father and we are His children. Puritan pastor John Owen said, "Having a loving fellowship with the Father is very much neglected by Christians . . . let us then see the Father full of love to us. Do not see the Father as one who is angry, but as one who is most kind and gentle."[2]

The fact that God is our heavenly Father is foundational to the Christian faith. Everything else flows from this great truth. Jesus said, "As the Father has loved me, so have I loved you" (John 15:9). The fatherhood of God is an amazing spiritual reality that is both humbling and life changing. God loves poor and lost sinners as a father loves his children. God loves you and me more than we can imagine or will ever know. If we never learned anything else about God, this would be enough. The Bible tells us:

> See how great a love the Father has bestowed on us, that we would be called children of God; and such we are. For this reason the world does not know us, because it did not know Him. Beloved, now we are children of God, and it has not appeared as yet what we will be. We know that when He appears, we will be like Him, because we will see Him just as He is. (1 John 3:1-2, NASB)

We are God's children and He is our Father: "You have received the Spirit of adoption as sons, by whom we cry, 'Abba! Father!'" (Romans 8:15). He is our Abba Father, which literally means "daddy" in Aramaic. In other words, our relationship with God should be personal, just like the relationship between a father and his child. We are God's adopted children in Christ Jesus, through whom we have become spiritual sons and daughters (see Galatians 3:26).

I have come to realize that God is my Father, not just in theory but in reality. I cannot think of any greater privilege or honor than to be considered a child of the living God. Think about it for a minute. The God of all creation is your heavenly Father. You and I are children of the God of the universe! Not only can we call Him Father, but we are told to call Him "Daddy."

GOING DEEPER: Why Know Doctrine?

A doctrine is spiritual truth from the Bible. Why should believers study doctrine? Doctrine matters because our doctrine influences what we think, and that affects how we live. Although we are not all called to be theologians, every Christian can learn basic doctrine.

While doctrine can seem stuffy, boring, and useless, it can also be surprisingly devotional. Yes, the study of God can profoundly deepen your faith and strengthen your relationship with the living God because doctrine helps us know more about Him. The more we know about Him, the more we love Him.

Sound doctrine gives us a foundation for our faith by helping us learn more about God (see 1 Timothy 4:16). We cannot fully know God without the study of God. Doctrine helps us grow in our faith because the more we know, the more we grow. Paul tells us that we should be "nourished in the words of faith and of the good doctrine" (1 Timothy 4:6, NKJV). Doctrine corrects us when we are wrong and in sin (see 2 Timothy 3:16).

TO HIM BE THE GLORY

The Apostles' Creed says that God is "almighty." Think about how great God really is. He is the real thing; there is no one like Him. To know God is to know that He is truly awesome and almighty. He is bigger, greater, and more amazing than we have ever imagined.

Think of how full of wonder you feel in the presence of a great mountain or looking at the stars in the sky, and then remind yourself that God is the One who created all that grandeur and majesty. J. I. Packer brings it into perspective, saying, "The true God is great and terrible, just because He is always with me and His eye is always upon me. Living becomes an awesome business when you realize that you spend every moment of your life in the sight and company of an omniscient, omnipresent Creator."[3] God's ways are above our ways and His thoughts are above our thoughts (see Isaiah 55:8). Paul says,

Oh, the depth of the riches both of the wisdom and knowledge of God! How unsearchable are His judgments and His ways past finding out!

> *"For who has known the mind of the LORD?*
> *Or who has become His counselor?*
> *Or who has first given to Him*
> *And it shall be repaid to him?"*

For of Him and through Him and to Him are all things, to whom be glory forever. Amen. (Romans 11:33-36, NKJV)

It's humbling to think about how small we are in comparison to all eternity. We are like a drop in the vast expanse of the ocean of time and space. Or as the Bible says, "What is your life? You are a mist that appears for a little while and then vanishes" (James 4:14, NIV). No matter how hard we try, we can't understand everything about God, because we are finite and He is infinite (see Isaiah 55:8). Neither can we put God under a microscope or examine Him as if He were subject to our scrutiny. But we can know some things about the Lord from His attributes as revealed in Scripture and nature.

The Bible tells us that God is all-wise and all-knowing. He knows all things, including the thoughts and intents of the heart. He is omniscient, which is the capacity to know everything infinitely.[4] He is intimately aware of everything that happens to every living thing (see Hebrews 4:13). The writer of the Psalms reflects on God's omniscience, saying, "How precious to me are your thoughts, O God! How vast is the sum of them!" (Psalm 139:17).

While it is impossible for us to be in more than one place at a time, it's not so with God. He is neither bound by time or space. He is omnipresent, which means He is everywhere at all times.[5] You may ask how this is possible. God is omnipresent in and through His Holy Spirit. The Bible says, "Where shall I go from your Spirit? Or where shall I flee from your presence?" (Psalm 139:7). Jesus promises, "For where two or three are gathered in my name, there am I among them" (Matthew 18:20). The promise of God's presence can be a great comfort in the life of a believer. No matter where you are or what you are doing, He is already there, waiting for you. Despite our outward circumstances, the Lord is always with us through the power and presence of the Holy Spirit.

God is all-powerful and mighty; nothing is too hard for Him (see Jeremiah 32:17). He is able to do far more abundantly than all that we ask or think (see Ephesians 3:20). Simply put, God can do anything. Many of us are guilty of having a small view of God. We need to step back and enlarge our understanding of the greatness and majesty of our God. Charles Misner, a scientific specialist, makes a provocative observation about Albert Einstein's skepticism of the church:

> The design of the universe . . . is very magnificent and shouldn't be taken for granted. In fact, I believe that is why Einstein had so little use for organized religion, although he strikes me as a basically very religious man. He must have looked at what the preachers said about God and felt they were blaspheming. He had seen much more majesty than they had ever imagined, and they were just not talking about the real thing. My guess is that he simply felt the religions he'd run across did not have proper respect . . . for the author of the universe.[6]

THE GREAT ARTIST

Life is like a story. As artists use their brush or authors use their pen to create, so God is the Author of the story in which we live. He spoke the world into existence. He is the great Artist who created by His word and for His glory: land, sea, and every living thing, including men and women. Everything in creation bears His mark and workmanship. He cares for and is continuously involved in His creation. God is aware of everything in His own creation, down to the smallest ant.

There are ecological and environmental implications of the doctrine of knowing that God is the divine Creator. If God is a magnificent Artist who created the earth in all of its majesty and splendor, don't you think we should appreciate and care for it? As Christians, we have a divine responsibility to care for the environment and creation. God created us to have dominion over the earth, not to destroy it. We are to be good stewards of this great planet.

When Christians have a robust understanding of creation, it helps us understand that we are called to environmental stewardship. Believers are beginning to answer the call for environmental stewardship through activities such as recycling and organizing community cleanups. There are many ways that we can practice environmental stewardship. Our church has adopted a beach access to clean on a monthly basis in order to practice environmental stewardship, and to show that we care about God's creation. This is a powerful witness to the unchurched. Evangelical Environmental Network is a ministry that seeks to educate, inspire, and mobilize Christians in their effort to care for God's creation.[7] I encourage you to take personal responsibility to care for God's creation and to be a faithful steward of God's earth.

PROFILES: Meet Patrick of Ireland (387–493)

Saint Patrick was one of the most influential Christians in the history of the Christian church.

Patrick was instrumental in the conversion of thousands, ordaining hundreds of clergy, and establishing many churches and monasteries. As a result of his ministry, Christianity spread like wildfire through

Ireland and into other parts of the British Isles. A humble missionary, he personally baptized over 100,000 people, driving paganism from the shores of Ireland and starting a movement in Ireland that helped preserve Christianity during the Middle Ages.

The churches and monasteries he established became some of the most influential missionary centers in all of Europe. Missionaries went out from Ireland to spread the gospel throughout the world. Saint Columba (521–597) established the famous monastery on the Isle of Iona. Irish monasteries helped preserve the Christian faith during the Dark Ages.

Patrick and the Celtic Christians had a profound appreciation for nature and creation. They saw God's beauty and majesty in creation, as seen in portions of this famous prayer, "Saint Patrick's Breastplate":

> I rise today
> in heaven's might,
> in sun's brightness,
> in moon's radiance,
> in fire's glory,
> in lightning's quickness,
> in wind's swiftness,
> in sea's depth,
> in earth's stability,
> in rock's fixity.
> I rise today
> in the power's strength, invoking the Trinity,
> believing in threeness,
> confessing the oneness,
> of creation's Creator.[8]

WORSHIP: OUR RESPONSE TO GOD

It's not long before we have to ask ourselves the question, If God is who He says He is, what should we do, and how should we live? The doctrine of God calls us to devotion, praise, and worship. There is a direct connection between our doctrine and devotion, because the knowledge of God produces true worship of God. God has revealed Himself in the Bible so that people will worship Him.

John 4:23-24 says, "But the hour is coming, and is now here, when the true worshipers will worship the Father in spirit and truth, for the Father is seeking such people to worship him. God is spirit, and those who worship him must worship in spirit and truth." God seeks people who will worship Him in spirit and truth. Believers have a responsibility to worship God in this way. He alone is worthy of our worship. God only receives sincere worship that comes from a pure heart. We should worship Him in spirit, which involves everything within us.

We were created to glorify and know the God who created us. Peter tells us that we "are a chosen generation, a royal priesthood, a holy nation, His own special people, that you may proclaim the praises of Him who called you out of darkness into His marvelous light" (1 Peter 2:9, NKJV). Christian worship is the fruit of our salvation and begins in our hearts as we give adoration and praise to God, and then it manifests outwardly as we lift up our voices to Him in prayer, praise, and song. Worship is the act of giving all of ourselves back to God. The English word means "worthship" and carries the idea of worthiness. God is worthy of our highest praise and worship.

REFLECT AND RESPOND

You and I need God. We were created to have fellowship with the Father of all creation, the Storyteller, and the great Artist. The Bible says, "Oh, taste and see that the LORD is good!" (Psalm 34:8). How comforting and sweet it is to know that God is our Father and is always looking down on us!

Do you know God as your loving heavenly Father? Take a moment to reflect on His greatness and His love for you. Think about the specific ways that He has provided for you over the years. Reflect on what He is doing in your life now. God is not only your Father, but the Father of the entire world. He cares for all of His creation from the greatest to the least.

1. America has become a pluralistic society where God means different things to different people. What does the Bible tell us about the uniqueness of God?
2. What does the Apostles' Creed tell us about the nature and character of God?
3. What specific things, in this chapter about God, stand out to you? Do any of them challenge or stretch your understanding of God?
4. What are some of the common misconceptions about God that are prevalent in our culture?
5. Think for a minute about God as your heavenly Father. Describe in your own words what it means to have God as your Father.
6. Do you believe that God is sovereign and in control over your life, our nation, and the future? If so, how should that affect the way we live our everyday lives?

CHAPTER 3

JESUS CHRIST: The Man Behind the Movement

The most pressing question on the problem of faith is whether a man as a civilized being can believe in the divinity of the Son of God, Jesus Christ, for therein rests the whole of our faith.

FYODOR DOSTOEVSKY

FEW PEOPLE, NO matter what they believe or who they are, would deny that Jesus Christ is one of the most significant men who ever walked the earth. He is, at once, the most loved and the most hated man in all of history. Wars have been waged in His name and millions of people have lost their lives for following Him. Over two thousand years ago, He inspired a revolutionary movement that has grown to include over two billion people from around the world.

Who is Jesus, really? Many both inside and outside the church are more confused than ever about who Jesus is. Some people view Him as a prophet, while others simply view Him as a good teacher. Great men, such as Thomas Jefferson, have denied the divinity of Jesus by saying, "Jesus did not mean to impose himself on mankind as the son of God." Along with others, Gandhi believed that, "He is as divine as Krishna or Rama or Muhammad or Zoroaster."[1]

Sadly, most people come to their own conclusions about Jesus without ever looking at what the Bible actually says about Him. Even worse, they look to movies such as *Jesus Christ Superstar, The Last Temptation of Christ*, and *The Da Vinci Code* or television shows such as *Joan of Arcadia* to influence their views about Him.

That's why it is more important than ever for Christians to really know about Jesus. In the next few pages, I want to paint a picture of Jesus and invite you to search, study, seek, and know Him for yourself.

THE STORY OF JESUS

As a small child, I thought about Jesus only around Christmastime. The Nativity scene was one of my favorite things to play with. I especially loved the camels and baby Jesus. I remember asking the little baby Jesus to make sure that I got my favorite toys for Christmas. I usually got the toys I asked for—not because I prayed to baby Jesus, but because I made sure that I covered all my bases by writing Santa Claus, too!

Unless they're from another planet, most North Americans know something about the story of Jesus, even if their only information is from a Christmas play or Nativity scene. The story of Jesus begins in a small town called Nazareth, when an angel appears to a virgin girl named Mary. The angel proceeds to tell her that she will conceive a child who will be the Son of God and that she should name Him Jesus. As you can imagine, Mary is blown away by the news, but the angel assures her that God will be with her. After nine months, Jesus is born in Bethlehem of Judea, near Jerusalem. He is born in a humble manger in a barn among the animals.

Jesus' birth was the most significant event in history because it was the day that God became a man. The God of the universe entered our world and humbled Himself to become one of us. The holy mystery is that Jesus actually became a man, yet remained fully God. As a man,

He was born, was part of a family, went through childhood and puberty, had to obey His parents, got hungry, thirsty, and worked as a carpenter. He experienced happiness, sadness, temptation, and compassion. He even got angry.[2] As the Son of God, He forgave sins and healed the sick, He was sinless, He received worship, and He said that He was the only way to heaven.[3]

GOING DEEPER: Defending the Incarnation

The birth of Jesus is also known as the Incarnation, which means "to become flesh." The word *incarnation* describes the divinity and humanity of Jesus. Early Christians sought to protect the church from heresies that denied the humanity and divinity of Jesus.

Athanasius (293–373) was an important early church leader of the fourth century. He is best remembered for his role as defender of the Incarnation in the conflict with Arius and Arianism. Arius taught that Jesus was a created being and therefore less than God. At the First Council of Nicaea, Athanasius argued against this view. The issue at stake was salvation, because Jesus had to be fully God and fully human in order for His sacrificial death to atone for our sins.

Find the Athanasian Creed on page 126 in the appendix.

Jesus' short ministry started when He was thirty years old and ended three years later. Thousands of people followed Jesus to hear His teachings and to witness His miracles. He often used parables to explain deep spiritual truths when teaching the multitudes of people that followed Him. He also spoke in the common everyday language of the people so they could understand Him. Many of these teachings and miracles are recorded in the four gospels of the New Testament.

Even though Jesus ministered to crowds of thousands, His real ministry was to a few select men called the disciples. Author Robert Coleman tells us that Jesus' ministry plan "was not with programs to reach the multitudes but with men whom the multitudes would follow. Men were to be His method of winning the world to God. The initial objective of Jesus' plan was to enlist men who could bear witness to His life and carry on His work after He returned to the Father."[4]

Jesus did not choose everyone He met to be His disciples. Rather than focusing on large numbers of people, He chose only twelve. His selectivity was intentional. Jesus' master plan was to instruct and train a few men who would reproduce themselves in others.

Religious leaders hated Jesus because they felt threatened by His growing popularity among the crowds (see Matthew 26:1-5). They made false statements about Him and demanded that Pontius Pilate, the Roman judge, sentence Jesus to die. He was thrown into a prison and Roman soldiers brutally beat Him with a whip until His flesh was torn and blood ran down His back. Jesus was nearly beaten to death.[5]

As if this punishment were not enough, He was then forced to carry His own wooden cross down the back streets of Jerusalem and up the hill to Golgotha. He was nailed to a cross of rough wood that was thrust into the ground. As Jesus hung on the cross, dying a slow and painful death, people mocked and scorned Him for calling Himself the Son of God.

The scene must have been horrific. As He died slowly on the cross, Jesus asked, "Father, forgive them, for they know not what they do" (Luke 23:34). Then in a final gasp He announced, "It is finished!" The instant He died, the sky was dark as night and the heavy veil of the temple was torn in half from the top down.

His broken and bloody body was taken down from the cross and buried in a borrowed tomb. The Romans assigned soldiers to guard Jesus' grave because the Jews were afraid that someone would steal His body. To prevent this from happening, a heavy stone was rolled across the tomb, and it was sealed shut. The Bible says that after three days Jesus rose from the dead, and the grave. When some of His followers came to the tomb to care for His body and found the tomb empty, they were afraid. Jesus then appeared to them outside the tomb saying, "Rejoice!" (Matthew 28:9, NKJV). Jesus' resurrection came as a great comfort to His disciples because they had seen Him die a cruel death.

The Resurrection is the point in the story of Jesus where some people depart from the road of classic Christianity. They believe that Jesus was a good man sent by God, but that the Resurrection is an absurd myth. However, the resurrection of Jesus Christ is one of the hallmarks of the Christian faith. The Bible says, "If Christ has not been raised, then our preaching is in vain and your faith is in vain" (1 Corinthians 15:14). The apostle Paul summed up the life, death, and resurrection of Jesus by saying, "Christ died for our sins in accordance with the Scriptures, that he was buried, that he was raised on the third day in accordance with the Scriptures, and that he appeared to Cephas, then to the twelve" (1 Corinthians 15:3-5).

After His resurrection, Jesus ascended into heaven (see Acts 1:9-11). He sits at God's right hand and intercedes for His people and rules as Lord over all. The Resurrection and the Ascension are comforting to Christians since we can know that because He lives and will return, we will one day be with Him again. There is an old song that says, "Because He lives, I can face tomorrow."[6]

That is the story of Jesus in a nutshell. Now let's consider His name.

WHAT'S IN A NAME?

We can learn a lot about people from their names. Some people are named after a relative or someone famous or because of the meaning behind the name itself. For instance, I was named after Winfield Dunn, the governor of Tennessee the year I was born, because my dad was serving as his campaign manager.

Throughout the Bible, men and women were given names that had specific spiritual significance and meaning. Some were named for good things and some for bad. Their names gave insight into who they were. Adam, the name of the first man, means "of the ground." Abraham means "father of a multitude." The name Peter means "rock." Delilah means "dainty one." Or how about the name Ichabod, which means "God has departed"?

Jesus' name and titles also have spiritual significance and meaning that are helpful for understanding who He is. The Apostles' Creed summarizes His names as "Jesus Christ, his only Son, our Lord." Like three different portraits of the same person, these three titles help us see Jesus from different perspectives, giving us a fuller picture of who He is. Let's take a closer look at each of them.

Jesus Christ

Jesus is one of the most well-known names in all of history. The name comes from the Hebrew word *Yeshua,* which means "Jehovah saves." Matthew 1:21 tells us, "She will bear a son, and you shall call his name Jesus, for he will save his people from their sins." God the Father sent Jesus to save humankind from sin and death. His name *Yeshua,* "Jehovah saves," perfectly describes why He came. He is our Jesus, who has come to save you and me from our sins.

The second name, *Christ,* is not Jesus' last name; it is a title given to Him to describe His prophetic role in God's redemptive plan. Hundreds of years before Jesus' birth, prophets predicted the coming of a Jewish Messiah. The Old Testament contains more than three hundred such prophecies pertaining to His miraculous birth, sinless life, miracles, death, and resurrection. Scripture shows us that Jesus is the Messiah of the Old and New Testaments, meaning He was specifically chosen by God to bring redemption and salvation to the world. The Hebrew word for Messiah means "chosen one" or "anointed one." The word *Messiah* is *Christ* in the New Testament Greek language, implying that Jesus is the fulfillment of all of the Old Testament prophecies about the Messiah.

Son of God

You cannot fully know Jesus unless you know that He is God's one and only Son. While we are all God's children, the Bible tells us that there is only one Son of God—Jesus Christ. When we understand that Jesus is God's Son, it helps us realize the awesome significance of their special relationship. To know Jesus is to know the Father, and vice versa, because they are one. Jesus said, "I and My Father are one" (John 10:30, NKJV).

Having children has helped me better understand the profound reality of the Father and His Son's divine relationship. My girls are a part of me and I am a part of them too. One of my daughters looks just like me. People call her "Mini Winnie" because she is a mini version of me. In the same way, we can see the Father in Jesus, the Son. He said, "Anyone who has seen me has seen the Father" (John 14:9, NIV).

Our Lord

Jesus is also called Lord. This title affirms the lordship of Jesus Christ and literally means that He is God. On many occasions Jesus accepted worship and forgave sins, which only God can do. For example, Luke 5 tells about a crippled man who is lowered through the roof so Jesus can heal him. When He sees the man, Jesus says, "Your sins are forgiven you" (verse 20). Scripture also tells us that the Pharisees "were seeking . . . to kill [Jesus] because . . . he was even calling God his own Father, making himself equal with God" (John 5:18). Without a doubt, Jesus claimed to be God. In addition, the Bible tells us that Jesus was with God in the beginning of Creation (see John 1:1,14), that "He is the image of the invisible God" (Colossians 1:15), and in Him "all the fullness of the Deity lives in bodily form" (Colossians 2:9, NIV). There can be no doubt that the writers of the New Testament believed that this man Jesus was both Lord and God.

PROFILES: Meet John Wesley (1703–1791)

John Wesley founded the Methodist movement. With skill and discipline, he quickly became one of the most influential leaders of the evangelical awakening of the eighteenth century. More than two hundred years have passed, and Wesley's life, message, and ministry still speak with the same power and relevance that they did then. Few men have left such an indelible mark upon church history.

Throughout his lifetime, Wesley traveled more than 250,000 miles, preached over 40,560 sermons, organized hundreds of Bible societies, built several schools, and so impacted Methodism that at the time of his death nearly 43,265 members and 198 ministers had been attracted to the movement.[7]

On May 24, 1738, while attending a prayer meeting at Aldersgate Street in London, John Wesley had a life-changing experience. He wrote:

> In the evening, I went very unwillingly to a society in Aldersgate Street, where one was reading Luther's Preface to the Epistle to the Romans. About a quarter before nine, while he was describing the change which God works in the heart through faith in Christ, I felt my heart strangely warmed. I felt I did trust in Christ, Christ alone for salvation; and an assurance was given me that he had taken away my sins, even mine, and saved me from the law of sin and death.[8]

FINDING FAITH IN JESUS

Jesus began His ministry with the declaration "The time is fulfilled. . . . Repent and believe in the gospel" (Mark 1:15). According to the Bible, we must repent and believe in Jesus as God. The word *repent* simply means to "turn" or "change one's mind." Repentance happens when Jesus calls us to turn from our waywardness in total surrender to God and live the life He has planned for us. In order to follow Jesus, we must be willing to change.

The second component of Mark 1:15, believing the gospel, means to trust God and His Word—to have faith that what He tells us is true, even though we're not given all the answers.

I think the reason faith is so hard for many people is because it is so simple. Jesus reminds us, "Whoever does not receive the kingdom of God as a little child will by no means enter it" (Mark 10:15, NKJV). Children don't need to be convinced; they just believe. The old children's hymn says it best: "Jesus loves me! This I know, for the Bible tells me so." Paul puts it into perspective by telling us, "If you confess with your mouth the Lord Jesus and believe in your heart that God has raised Him from the dead, you will be saved" (Romans 10:9, NKJV).

Let me tell you Adam's story. Adam is a young schoolteacher who did not grow up going to church. The few times that he did attend a church, he was exposed to bad church politics, and so he came to believe that most Christians were hypocrites. Sadly, he was exposed to religion—not to a relationship with Jesus—and he wanted nothing to do with church.

Adam always considered himself a good guy who never really did anything bad. Then he and his wife attended our first Christmas service at Church of the Outer Banks. That morning I was preaching a sermon called "From the Cradle to the Cross" on the significance of the birth of Jesus. At the conclusion, I invited everyone to respond to the message by accepting Jesus into his or her heart. That day Adam gave his heart to Jesus Christ, and his life was forever changed. Today he is still walking with Jesus, and he is an important leader in our church.

Adam's story isn't unique. I have met hundreds of people from all over the United States and around the world who have put their faith and hope in Jesus Christ. These people come from different backgrounds and stages in life. Some are poor and others are millionaires.

What each of them has in common is a simple faith and trust in Jesus Christ as their Lord and Savior.

When Jesus calls a person, He demands a response. The call of God is one that cannot be ignored or unanswered. Either the hearer will trust and obey, or doubtfully deny. It is up to us to answer and to respond to the call. Dietrich Bonhoeffer said, "When Christ calls a man, he bids him come and die."[9] In this sense, it is a call to total self-surrender. We are still expected to leave everything to follow Jesus, just as the disciples did in their day.

In the end, a person must either accept the claims of the Bible in faith or dismiss them entirely. C. S. Lewis wrote,

> A man who was merely a man and said the sort of things Jesus said would not be a great moral teacher. He would either be a lunatic—on the level with a man who says he is a poached egg—or he would be the Devil of Hell. You must make your choice. Either this man was, and is, the Son of God: or else a madman or something worse. You can shut Him up for a fool, you can spit at Him and kill Him as a demon; or you can fall at His feet and call Him Lord and God. But let us not come with any patronizing nonsense about His being a great human teacher. He has not left that open to us. He did not intend to.[10]

REFLECT AND RESPOND

How then are we to respond to Jesus? Each one of us must decide for ourselves whether Jesus is Lord, a liar, or a lunatic. Either He is the Son of God, or He is not. I have known many wonderful people who have wanted to believe in Jesus, but simply could not affirm His divinity.

Every journey begins with the first step. Becoming a Christian is simple, yet deeply profound. It begins with God's free offer of salvation through His Son, Jesus Christ. If you are not a believer, all you need to do is put your faith and hope in Jesus Christ as Lord and Savior. Trust in Him alone to save you from your sin and fallen nature by what He has already done for you on the cross. Surrender your life to Him today and begin to follow Him.

Being a follower of Jesus is not for the faint of heart. It doesn't mean you'll never have another problem or difficulty in your life. In fact, as a believer you may actually have to suffer for your faith. All Christians are called to identify with Christ's mission, which sometimes involves suffering and death. This does not mean that we will necessarily have to die for our faith, but we must be willing and ready to lay down our lives for the Lord. As disciples of Jesus, we must be willing to accept whatever may come our way as a result of the mission and message of Christ.

1. Jesus is the most loved and hated man who has ever walked the planet. What unique claims does Christianity have about the person and divinity of Jesus Christ?

2. What does the name Jesus tell us about God's redemptive plan for humanity? How does that fit within the overall picture of God's Story?

3. Jesus is the Christ, which means He is the Jewish Messiah. What does this tell us about the historical significance of Jesus?

4. What does the Bible say about Jesus as the unique one and only Son of God? How is that different from our being God's created sons and daughters?

5. The Apostles' Creed says Jesus Christ is "our Lord." This means that He is Lord and God. What are the implications of the lordship of Jesus?

6. How did you come to know Jesus? If you have never had a personal encounter with Christ, take some time to reflect on how you should respond to the gospel message.

CHAPTER 4

THE HOLY SPIRIT:
Give Me That Old-Time Religion

Because we have shut out the Holy Spirit in so many ways, we are stumbling along as though we are spiritually blindfolded.

A. W. TOZER

WE NEED THE Holy Spirit to live the Christian life, yet somewhere along the way, the church has forgotten about the Holy Spirit. The Spirit is neglected in many Christians' lives, as well as in churches across our nation. Somehow we began to do things in our own power and strength instead of relying on God. Many churches focus more on buildings and budgets than on seeking God's powerful presence through prayer. Consequently, churches across the country are dying and desperately in need of spiritual renewal because they have lost the presence and power of the Holy Spirit.

You may be wondering, *Who or what in the world is the Holy Spirit?* Christians have been asking similar questions about the Spirit since the time of Christ. Jesus' promise to send us the Holy Spirit is one of the most mysterious and misunderstood promises of Scripture. There have been many different opinions about the person and work of the Holy Spirit. Some people think the Spirit is just a created being, while others believe that the Spirit is merely an impersonal energy force.

But if you take a step back and read through the pages of the book of Acts, you will see that the Holy Spirit played an important role in the life and ministry of the early church. You can't read the story of the early church without seeing the church's overwhelming reliance on the power of the Holy Spirit. Jesus' last words to those early believers were, "You will receive power when the Holy Spirit has come upon you" (Acts 1:8). The explosive growth of the early church was due to the dynamic power and presence of the Holy Spirit in the lives of believers.

We need some of that old-time religion! You don't have to be super-spiritual to be open to the Spirit in your life. There is a growing hunger among ordinary Christians who want to experience the Holy Spirit in their everyday lives. Today a fresh renewal of the Holy Spirit is taking place in churches, denominations, and networks across the country, and around the world.

"I BELIEVE IN THE HOLY SPIRIT"

The Apostles' Creed simply affirms, "I believe in the Holy Spirit." Although short and sweet, this statement reminds us of the central and important role that the Spirit has in salvation, discipleship, church renewal, and the spread of the gospel today. Without the Spirit, it is impossible to experience spiritual renewal in your life or church. The doctrine of the Holy Spirit has an important contribution to make in the contemporary church today.

I invite you to open your heart and mind to find out more about the person and work of the Spirit for yourself. We can benefit from studying about the Holy Spirit because learning more about Him and His work will enable us to experience Him in a deeper way in our lives and our churches. To clear up some of the confusion, let's begin by looking at the person of the Holy Spirit.

MEET THE HOLY SPIRIT

Some people deny the divinity and even the existence of the Holy Spirit. However, the Bible clearly emphasizes the divinity of the Holy Spirit.[1] In other words, the Holy Spirit is God. There is a unique relationship between God the Father; Jesus Christ, the Son; and the Holy Spirit. This interrelationship is called the Trinity, which refers to three distinct divine personalities, each wholly God, yet one in essence. The doctrine of the Trinity has been defended by the Christian church for nearly two thousand years. Another one of the earliest doctrinal statements of the Christian faith called the Nicene Creed beautifully describes the divinity of the Holy Spirit: "And we believe in the Holy Spirit, the Lord, the giver of life. He proceeds from the Father and the Son, and with the Father and the Son is worshiped and glorified. He spoke through the prophets."[2]

The Holy Spirit has a personal nature and can be known by believers in an intimate way. Sadly, many people think of the Spirit as a mysterious and impersonal power source, like electricity. For this reason some Christians find it hard to understand the Spirit's personal nature and refer to the Spirit as an "it." In contrast, the Bible ascribes personal characteristics to the Spirit.[3] For instance, the Spirit has a will (see Acts 13:2; 1 Corinthians 12:11), a mind (see 1 Corinthians 2:10-11; Romans 8:27), and emotions (see Ephesians 4:30).

Jesus called the Holy Spirit the Comforter, which means one who is called alongside us in our troubles (see John 14:16,26). The Bible never says that adversity and suffering will not come into our lives, but it does say that God is always with us in the midst of our times of greatest need through the comforting presence of the Holy Spirit (see 2 Corinthians 1:3-4). Even in the midst of trials, suffering, and sorrow, "God is our refuge and strength, an ever-present help in trouble" (Psalm 46:1, NIV).

I have some close friends whose father recently passed away after battling cancer for several months. Rather than doubting God, the family actually drew closer to Him. Throughout the process I witnessed the comforting Holy Spirit work in the lives of each family member. I vividly remember talking to the father on the phone one afternoon shortly before his death. His last words to me were, "I know that God is real, and I am ready to go to my heavenly home." His assurance put tears in my eyes and joy in my heart. Maybe you are facing a difficult or painful situation. If so, let the Holy Spirit come alongside you.

PROFILES: Meet John Owen (1616–1683)

The English Puritans started a movement in the sixteenth and seventeenth centuries that sought to purify the Church of England in worship and doctrine. It was the outgrowth of the Reformation and heavily influenced the later development of Christianity in North America. The Puritans placed a special emphasis on the transforming work of the Holy Spirit in salvation, which strongly influenced modern evangelicalism.

Puritan theologians wrote extensive works on the person and work of the Holy Spirit. John Owen, a leading Puritan pastor and theologian, wrote the book *The Holy Spirit: His Gifts and Power*. Owen served as a chaplain to Oliver Cromwell and later became Dean of Christ Church in the University of Oxford.

Owen said, "We have communion with the Holy Spirit in his willingness to be the Comforter and helper. The Spirit willingly proceeds from the Father and the Son in this work of salvation. He is as willing to take upon himself the work of comforter and helper as the Son was willing to take on himself the work of redeemer."[4]

HOW THE SPIRIT WORKS

Once you discover the Holy Spirit for yourself, it is important to find out how the Spirit desires to work in your life. The Spirit is not just a truth or a fact to be known, but an important part of the triune Godhead who works in us and through us so that we become the men and women that God has called us to be. We don't just need to know about the Holy Spirit in theory, but we must experience Him in reality.

Being a Christian is more than a confession or a creed; it's a lifestyle and a way of life. God changes our hearts and our lives through the ongoing work of the Holy Spirit. We are to walk in the Spirit (see Galatians 5:16), meaning we are to daily surrender our lives and yield ourselves to the Spirit's influence and guidance. Life is tough sometimes, and we need the Spirit's indwelling presence to help us live for Christ.

One way we can determine the health of a plant or a tree is by looking at its fruit. The same is true when it comes to the health of our spiritual lives. Do we bear good fruit or bad fruit? Jesus said, "You will know them by their fruits" (Matthew 7:16, NKJV). In John 15:8, He promised that if we abide in Him, we will bear much spiritual fruit.

Galatians 5:22-23 lists nine Christian virtues that are collectively called the fruit of the Spirit that the Holy Spirit imparts to believers who abide in Christ: "love, joy, peace, patience, kindness, goodness, faithfulness, gentleness and self-control" (NIV). Paul uses the fruit of the Spirit to show the difference between someone who is walking by the Spirit and someone who is living for the world. The works of the flesh refer to sinful desires while the fruit of the Spirit is the hallmark of a Spirit-filled life. Spiritual fruit is the natural overflow of a life that is abiding in Christ.

GOING DEEPER: The Fruit of the Spirit

Take a few minutes and look at the fruit of the Spirit in Galatians 5:22-23. As you read through the following list, ask the Holy Spirit to develop fruit in your life.

1. **Love.** What's love got to do with it? Everything. The Christian faith is all about love because "God is love" (1 John 4:16). This is the first and most important of all of the fruit of the Spirit. Love is sacrificial and seeks the good of others before oneself. Love finds its source from God alone.

2. **Joy.** Joy is a deep gladness that comes from a personal relationship with Jesus Christ. As Christians, everything we do should be done with joy in our hearts (see 1 Thessalonians 5:16). The joy of the Lord is our strength because it comes directly from Him (see Nehemiah 8:10). Joy is independent of our outward circumstances and should flow from the heart of every believer's life.

3. **Peace.** Peace is a spiritual well-being that only God can give. Jesus said, "Peace I leave with you; my peace I give to you. Not as the world gives do I give to you" (John 14:27). This doesn't mean you will never have another problem, but that God will give you peace in the midst of the storm. Let the peace of God fill your heart and soul through the power of the Spirit.

4. **Patience.** Patience means holding out in the midst of trials and difficulty. It is putting up with others, waiting through the difficult times, and not giving up even when we are severely tried. Having patience is like having a spiritual rubber band. When we are being stretched, we will not break if we possess long-suffering.

5. **Kindness.** Kindness is being able to respond to the needs of others who are hurting. Those who have experienced the

kindness of God's salvation in Christ are to demonstrate the same kindness toward others.

6. **Goodness.** Goodness is the generosity that overflows from kindness. Although goodness and kindness are similar, goodness is a more active term and is often directed toward others in a benevolent way. It is the action of helping others in need. We are to take action and become agents of God's goodness in the world. The virtue of goodness reminds us that we become the hands and feet of Jesus Christ.

7. **Faithfulness.** Faithfulness is one of the most common words in the New Testament and is used in a variety of ways. It refers to being a person who God and others can rely upon. When we look at the great men and women in the Bible, we see that they all shared one thing in common: They were faithful.

8. **Gentleness.** To be gentle doesn't mean that we are weak or anemic; on the contrary, it refers to controlled strength. Gentleness is closely associated with humility and means to be mild or tame. Jesus is a great example of gentleness. His willingness to die on the cross for us wasn't a sign of weakness; rather, it was a sign of great strength and sacrifice.

9. **Self-control.** We live in a world where people think they should do whatever they feel like doing, regardless of the consequences. Many people think, *If it feels good, do it.* Self-control is exactly the opposite. It means to deny yourself and your sinful desires. It is relying on the power of the Spirit to overcome the desires of the flesh.

A WORD ABOUT SPIRITUAL GIFTS

Any discussion of the Holy Spirit has to address the issue of spiritual gifts. It is important to note that godly men and women have different

views concerning the gifts of the Spirit and how they continue to oper-
ate today. Christians can and do disagree over this issue.[5] Cessationists
believe that the sign gifts (tongues, prophecy, and healing) ceased with
the time of the apostles, while Charismatics believe all the gifts of the
Spirit are in continual operation and that believers can claim possession
of spiritual gifts. Whether you are a Cessationist, Charismatic, or somewhere in between, you should be open to the Spirit's work in your life.

We may disagree on which gifts are for today, but we should all
agree that the Spirit continues to give spiritual gifts to God's people
for service. Since the beginning of time the Holy Spirit has given gifts
to men and women in order to accomplish God's plans and purposes.

So what are spiritual gifts? Spiritual gifts are not a natural ability,
hobby, or interest, or even a profession. Just because someone has a gift
of playing basketball or golf doesn't mean that it was supernaturally
given to that person by the Lord. Spiritual gifts are literally called
charisma, which means "grace gifts" in the Bible. Grace is a gift supernaturally given by the Spirit. Wayne Grudem defines a spiritual gift as
"any ability that is empowered by the Holy Spirit and used in any
ministry of the church."[6] However, we can and should use our natural
talents and abilities for the glory of God and the sake of the gospel.
Here are some key points the Bible teaches about spiritual gifts:

- The gifts of the Spirit are available to all believers
  (see 1 Corinthians 12:7,11).
- The main purpose of the gifts is to build up the body of Christ
  (see Ephesians 4:7-13), and to glorify God (see 1 Peter 4:10-11).
- Spiritual gifts are also given by the Holy Spirit to individual
  believers to empower and enable them to serve others
  (see 1 Corinthians 12:4-21; Ephesians 4:7-13; Romans 12:6-8).

The Holy Spirit is the One who gives the gifts as He wills
(see 1 Corinthians 12:11). The gifts are not the result of human effort,

but they are completely the work of the Holy Spirit. John Owen reminded us, "He works sovereignly. The Holy Spirit distributes to everyone as He wills. He gives one gift to one person and a different gift to another person. So the saints are kept in constant dependence on him and his sovereignty."[7] Affirming God's sovereignty over the gifts keeps us humble and dependent upon Him.

EXPERIENCING THE HOLY SPIRIT

Have you ever had a real encounter with the Holy Spirit? By this I mean something that is as real as the sun shining on your face, the summer breeze blowing through your hair, or the sand in your toes. Sound crazy? It's true. You can experience the fullness of the Holy Spirit in your life. I believe that the Holy Spirit is available for all Christians to experience today. The Spirit wants to bring each of us into a deeper, more intimate relationship with Christ.

I am not writing as a theologian, but as an ordinary guy whose life has been deeply touched and impacted by the Holy Spirit's work. Like everyone else, I have had my fair share of struggles, doubts, and fears over the years. When I became a believer I was a little raw and rough around the edges. I needed the Lord to give me the strength and power to overcome my sinful desires and old lifestyle that were contrary to my new life in Christ. I didn't need to just know about the truth; I needed to experience it for myself, firsthand.

Then one night it happened. I had my first encounter with the Holy Spirit while attending a young-adult retreat in the beautiful mountains of east Tennessee. The Spirit of the Lord came into my life in an amazing way and began to give me the strength I needed to continue to walk out the Christian life in faith. I left that retreat with a renewed sense of God's presence and victory in my life. My life has never been the same since that night, and I continue to seek to walk in the Spirit every day.

HE WILL BE YOUR GUIDE

Many people have no sense of purpose or direction and live their lives as if they were playing Russian roulette. This is one of the reasons why there is so much chaos and disorder in people's lives. But it doesn't have to be this way for Christians. We are not left to figure things out on our own; God is with us. The Holy Spirit wants to guide and direct us in everything that we do.

Jesus said, "When He, the Spirit of truth, has come, He will guide you into all truth" (John 16:13, NKJV). The Spirit is a Guide who leads us in the way we should live our lives. I am confident that it is God's deepest desire that we seek His wisdom and will in every area of our lives.

I regularly take time out of each day to ask the Holy Spirit to guide me. I begin by praying each morning, *Holy Spirit, lead and guide me today.* He will guide you, too, if you will ask and be open to His leading. Listen for God's voice to speak into your life. God usually doesn't speak in an audible voice from heaven, but in the quiet, still voice of God. It is as faint as a whisper, and if we are not careful, we will miss it.

It can be tough to know when God is speaking to us, and when it is our own desires or thoughts, so here are some guidelines that you can use to discern when God is speaking to you.

1. The Holy Spirit speaks through the Word of God. The more you can get into the Word, the more God will speak to you through His Word. He uses the Bible to reveal His will for our lives and will never speak anything that is contrary to it. The Holy Spirit never draws attention to Himself, but always seeks to glorify Jesus.

2. God also speaks through ordinary, everyday events and circumstances. Never underestimate small things that happen from day to day because the Lord may be using them to speak to you. Other times He may speak through a still, small voice in your heart in prayer. A lot of people see prayer as a monologue rather than a dialogue. Don't just talk to God; stop and let Him talk to you. Be patient and listen.

3. God might use somebody else to speak to you, even when you least expect it. Sometimes God may use someone you already know; other times He may use a complete stranger. The Bible is full of stories and examples of how God speaks through others to share His word.[8]

Are you seeking God's will for your life or facing an important life-changing decision? Trust the Lord and His Word to show you the answer to all of life's problems and challenges. Don't be afraid to ask God for direction in your life. He speaks to those who are willing to ask and listen.

POWER TO BE A WITNESS

Many people are afraid to share their faith with others. Why is that? Why don't we share our faith? I think many times it's because of fear—*What will this person think of me?* The Bible says, "God has not given us a spirit of fear, but of power and of love and of a sound mind" (2 Timothy 1:7, NKJV). Here is another way that you can rely on the Holy Spirit. The Holy Spirit will help you move past all of your fears and share your faith with boldness.

At times we rely on our own persuasiveness instead of seeking the power of the Holy Spirit when telling someone about Christ. Instead, we need to ask the Spirit to fill us with His power so we can be effective witnesses. Jesus promised, "You shall receive power when the Holy Spirit has come upon you; and you shall be witnesses to Me" (Acts 1:8, NKJV). He promised us the power of the Spirit; all we have to do is ask for it and seek it. Pastor David Martyn Lloyd-Jones reminded us, "It is always right to seek the fullness of the Spirit—we are exhorted to do so."[9]

I have met too many weak and powerless Christians. Don't be ashamed to ask for the Holy Spirit to give you power to be a witness. In Acts the church prayed, "Grant to Your servants that with all boldness they may speak Your word," and when they finished praying, "they were all filled with the Holy Spirit, and they spoke the word of God with boldness" (Acts 4:29-31, NKJV). Ask the Lord for boldness, open your heart, and let the Holy Spirit give you power to be a witness for Christ today.

REFLECT AND RESPOND

I want to conclude this chapter with a call for us to invite the Spirit to have His way in our lives, our homes, and our churches. Perhaps the reason He doesn't do more in our churches is because we don't expect or even want Him to. Martyn Lloyd-Jones said, "We should always be open, in mind and in heart, to anything that the Spirit of God may choose to do in his sovereignty."[10] Are you open to the work of the Holy Spirit in your life or your church? Take some time to surrender your heart and your life to Him today. Ask Him to fill you today with His presence and give you the power and boldness to share your faith with others.

1. This chapter has offered an overview of the person and work of the Holy Spirit. Who or what is the Holy Spirit?
2. The Holy Spirit is both divine and a unique person within the Godhead. What personal experience have you had with the Holy Spirit?
3. What are some of the ways that the Bible describes the personal nature of the Holy Spirit? Why is it important to understand that the Holy Spirit has a personal nature?
4. What do the biblical names and titles of the Spirit tell us about who the Holy Spirit is? In what ways do they give you insight into the Spirit's nature?
5. What are some of the ways that the Holy Spirit has worked in your life in the past? How is the Spirit working in your life now?

CHAPTER 5

THE CHURCH: In Search of Community

The church is the only society in the world that exists for the benefit of those who are not yet its members.

WILLIAM TEMPLE, Archbishop of Canterbury

I LOVE THE local church with all of my heart, and I always will. However, this wasn't always the case. Before I was a Christian, church was one of the last places on earth I wanted to be. Like many people, I thought it was boring, dry, stuffy, and irrelevant. In a recent book entitled *They Like Jesus but Not the Church*, Dan Kimball addressed some people's negative view toward the church. Sadly, the book accurately assesses many people's attitudes.

Church is one of the last places many people look to find faith these days. Statistics show that many churches in North America are in decline. It's no secret that many of the mainline denominations in North America are dying rather than growing.[1] In *The American Church in Crisis,* David Olson discovered that only 17.5 percent of the United States population is attending a Christian church on any given weekend.[2]

To some extent, we who are a part of the church are responsible for some of the misunderstandings and misconceptions regarding church. Some churches in North America are still living in the past and look more like something from the 1940s than a twenty-first-century expression of Christ's body. Others have given in to the sin of pragmatism, focusing more on church growth than church health, and cultural accommodation rather than biblical faithfulness. Still other churches are more concerned about fighting one another than they are about reaching their neighborhoods for Christ. I think this reveals that many people (Christians and non-Christians) have a misunderstanding of the true nature of the church as a local expression of the body of Christ. It also reveals neglect on the part of some churches to reach out into the world around them.

Despite all of this, I still believe in the church. If there is one thing I know, there is no perfect church because people are not perfect. While there is no perfect church, there is a perfect Christ and the church is His body. In an article entitled, "The Church—Why Bother?" Tim Stafford says, "A living, breathing congregation is the only place to live in a healthy relationship to God. That is because it is the only place on earth where Jesus has chosen to dwell."[3] The church is God's plan for spiritual growth; there is no backup plan. Gene Getz says, "The more we understand God's wonderful plan for the church and the more we are involved in this process of spiritual growth, the more excited we will become about the church of Jesus Christ!"[4] I want to take the next few pages to answer the following questions: What is the church? What does the church do? Why does the church exist?

THE CHURCH IS THE BODY OF CHRIST

Today many people view the church as an organization or a building. This wasn't always the case. Slowly over time, people's concept of church shifted from being the people who gathered together in the name of Jesus to simply being a structure that is used on Sunday mornings. Nothing could be further from the truth. Nowhere in the New Testament does the word *church* refer to a building; in fact, there were no church buildings until three hundred years after the

time of Christ, when Christianity became the official religion of the
Roman Empire.

We need to rethink what it means in biblical terms to be the
church. A closer look reveals that the Old and New Testaments use
various organic metaphors to describe spiritual growth, such as sowing
and reaping (see John 4:37; 2 Corinthians 9:6), planting and watering
(see 1 Corinthians 3:6), growing (see 1 Peter 2:2; 2 Peter 3:18), and
bearing fruit (see Matthew 7:17-20; John 15:1-16; Galatians 5:22-23).
The church is a living and breathing organism. The apostle Paul talks
about the whole body as a metaphor for Christ's church, where every
member and part has an important role to play in the whole (see
1 Corinthians 12:12-27; Ephesians 4).

Jesus Christ is the head of the church, the body of Christ. Just as
the physical body has to have a structure to hold it together while
allowing it to grow and develop, the body of Christ has an organic
structure where each member has a role to play. If one member of the
body is out of place or is not working, the rest of the body suffers as a
result. The church is like a mosaic or tapestry that is made up of many
colors. Each piece contributes to making it a beautiful masterpiece. In
a similar way, the church is full of people from various backgrounds
who have different skills and talents that form one beautiful body of
Christ.

Another biblical metaphor for the church is a spiritual family. The
Bible uses terms like sister, brother, mother, father, bride, and husband
to refer to the relational nature of the Christian faith. As believers we
are spiritual brothers and sisters in Christ Jesus. My good friend Brad
always calls me his "brother from another mother." What he really
means is we are brothers in Christ, despite being from different parents
and living in different states.

THE CHURCH IS "CATHOLIC"

Let's look at the line in the Apostles' Creed that says "the holy catholic church." The word *catholic* does not specifically refer to the modern Catholic Church of Rome. It simply means "universal" and refers to the universal nature of the church. Paul reminds us, "There is one body and one Spirit . . . one Lord, one faith, one baptism, one God and Father of all" (Ephesians 4:4-6). There is only one true church, and it is made up of all true believers in Jesus Christ.

The universal nature of the church is a beautiful mystery and a profound truth of the Christian faith. Think about it for a minute. The church is universally made up of all true believers from every time, place, and part of the world. It transcends our geographical and language boundaries. Our God is a global God. Pastor and writer John Stott reminds us, "We must be global Christians with a global vision because our God is a global God."[5]

The Christian faith literally spans the world and is made up of millions of men and women who live in hundreds of countries and speak thousands of different languages. We are deeply connected to other believers from around the world. You and I may never meet these believers, but we are still a part of the same great family and body of Christ. I have brothers and sisters in Christ who live in Africa, China, and Russia. The Bible paints this beautiful picture of the global nature of the church:

> I looked, and behold, a great multitude that no one could number, from every nation, from all tribes and peoples and languages, standing before the throne and before the Lamb, clothed in white robes, with palm branches in their hands, and crying out with a loud voice, "Salvation belongs to our God who sits on the throne, and to the Lamb!" And all the angels were standing around the throne and around the elders and the four living creatures, and they fell on their faces before the throne and worshiped God, saying, "Amen!

Blessing and glory and wisdom and thanksgiving and honor
and power and might be to our God forever and ever! Amen."
(Revelation 7:9-12)

THE CHURCH IS LOCAL

Every believer should be a part of a local church because the church
universal is made up of local congregations of believers who gather
together in the name of Jesus Christ to worship, grow, and live out the
message of faith together. In the time of the New Testament there
were local churches throughout the cities of the Middle East in places
like Ephesus, Galatia, Corinth, and Philippi. Many of these early
churches were small in size and met in homes due to widespread
persecution.

Today we have many different expressions of the local church.
Some churches have buildings while others meet in homes. Some
churches meet in bowling alleys, funeral homes, YMCAs, schools, and
some even meet outdoors. Some churches are Anglican, Baptist,
Methodist, Presbyterian, or nondenominational. Some churches are
traditional, others are contemporary, and some are home fellowships.
The list could go on and on.

A commonality is that each congregation of believers is gathered
in a local expression of being the church wherever they are. The church
in Africa looks different than the church in Texas; each one is called
to be the church in its unique context and culture. One of the best
experiences of my life was spending a summer traveling across the
countryside of Peru. I was able to visit and worship with dozens of
different churches throughout the country—churches in cities,
jungles, and the Andes mountains. Each church was a little different;
however, they all had one thing in common: They worshipped Jesus
Christ.

PROFILES: Meet C. S. Lewis (1898–1963)

C. S. Lewis was an internationally known British author, scholar, lay theologian, and professor at Cambridge and Oxford universities. He was close friends with famed author J. R. R. Tolkien, who wrote *The Lord of the Rings* trilogy. Lewis wrote more than thirty books, including poetry, children's books, and numerous books on Christianity. He was concerned about divisions in the body of Christ and believed that Christians should be united in the essentials of the faith.

Lewis was once asked, "Is attendance at a place of worship or membership with a Christian community necessary to a Christian way of life?" His answer was as follows:

That's a question which I cannot answer. My own experience is that when I first became a Christian, about fourteen years ago, I thought that I could do it on my own, by retiring to my rooms and reading theology, and I wouldn't go to the churches and Gospel Halls; and then later I found that it was the only way of flying your flag; and, of course, I found that this meant being a target. It is extraordinary how inconvenient to your family it becomes for you to get up early to go to Church. It doesn't matter so much if you get up early for anything else, but if you get up early to go to Church it's very selfish of you and you upset the house. If there is anything in the teaching of the New Testament which is in the nature of a command, it is that you are obliged to take the Sacrament, and you can't do it without going to Church. I disliked very much their hymns, which I considered to be fifth-rate poems set to sixth-rate music. But as I went on I saw the great merit of it. I came up against different people of quite different outlooks and different education, and then gradually my conceit just began peeling off. I realized that the hymns (which were just sixth-rate music) were, nevertheless, being sung with devotion and benefit by an old saint in elastic-side boots in the opposite pew, and then you realize that you aren't fit to clean those boots. It gets you out of your solitary conceit.[6]

WHY DO THEY DO THAT?

I can remember being a little confused when I first began attending a local church because I observed several practices that seemed a little strange until I figured them out. Most Christian churches share certain practices, particularly water baptism and the Lord's Supper, regardless of their affiliation. These two practices are commonly referred to as sacraments or ordinances of the church. The term *ordinance* signifies that the acts of baptism and the Lord's Supper are ordained by Christ for the church, while the term *sacrament* literally means "mystery" and refers to an outward sign instituted by God to convey an inward or spiritual grace. Whatever you choose to call them, they are important and vital practices of the church. Let's take a closer look at each of these.

Water Baptism

Christian baptism is the immersion of a believer in water in the name of the Father, the Son, and the Holy Spirit. It is an act of obedience symbolizing the believer's newness of life in Christ Jesus. The Great Commission says that we are to "make disciples of all nations, baptizing them in the name of the Father and of the Son and of the Holy Spirit" (Matthew 28:19). The fact that baptism is included in the Great Commission demonstrates that it plays an important role in our discipleship and following Jesus Christ.

Baptism is the initiation into the Christian community and the first steps into the life of discipleship. Author Stephen Smallman says that baptism is the first phase of being a disciple.[7] A new believer should be baptized because Jesus was baptized, and He taught baptism (see Matthew 3:13-17). Baptism is a public display and confession of faith in the free gift of salvation by grace through faith in Jesus Christ as Savior and Lord (see Acts 2:38-39).

This is an amazing way for new Christians to feel accepted and loved by the Christian community. Baptism can be an important celebratory event in believers' lives, connecting them to the church family. Christians both old and new join together to celebrate the public declaration of faith of new believers.

At Church of the Outer Banks we make baptism a very special celebration. Several times a year we gather at the beach to perform ocean baptisms. After new believers are baptized, we offer them an olive wood cross to commemorate their experience and entry into the community of faith.

The Lord's Supper

The other common practice in evangelical churches is coming to the table of the Lord and taking the Lord's Supper. The Lord's Supper is a symbolic act where Christians memorialize the death of Jesus Christ and anticipate His second coming by eating small pieces of bread or wafers and drinking a sip of juice (or wine in some churches).[8] The Lord's Supper is also commonly referred to as *Communion* or the *Eucharist*. While baptism is a one-time initiatory rite, the Lord's Supper is a continuing practice that churches observe repeatedly. Professor John Hammett says, "The Lord's Supper is similar to an anniversary celebration in which wedding vows are renewed."[9]

In the midst of intimate community, early Christians shared the breaking of bread daily. We read in Acts 2:42, "They devoted themselves to the apostles' teaching and the fellowship, to the breaking of bread and the prayers." The breaking of bread was a continual reminder of what Christ did for them. It was also a reminder of God's continual presence and activity in the church: past, present, and future.

We are spiritually nourished as we share in the Lord's Supper. Christ supernaturally feeds us with His body and blood. John Wesley said, "Our bodies are strengthened by bread and wine, so are our souls by these tokens of the body and blood of Christ. This is the food of our souls: This gives strength to perform our duty and leads us on to perfection."[10] God's grace is given through the presence of the Holy Spirit as believers share in the memorial meal. Next time you take the Lord's Supper, reflect on the spiritual reality of what Christ has done for you through His life, death, and resurrection.

In a way the Lord's Supper is a picture of what heaven will be like because we are all one at Christ's table. At the table of the Lord our differences no longer matter. Young, old, black, white, rich, and poor are all welcome at the Supper.

GOING DEEPER: Reformation View of the Church

The Reformation was a reform movement in Europe that began in 1517. It began with Martin Luther and others as an attempt to reform the abuses and excesses of the Catholic Church. Many of the Reformers were troubled by what they saw as false doctrines and abuses within the Catholic Church.

The Reformation had a distinct view of the church and identified several unique marks of a healthy church, including preaching and administration of the sacraments. Established in 1563, one of the Thirty-Nine Articles of the Church of England says, "The visible Church of Christ is a congregation of faithful men, in which the pure word of God is preached, and the sacraments duly administered according to Christ's ordinance in all those things that of necessity are requisite to the same." In the *Institutes of the Christian Religion*, John Calvin said, "Wherever we see the Word of God purely preached *and heard*, and the sacraments administered according to Christ's institution, there, it is not to be doubted, a church of God exists."[11]

Okay, we've talked about what the church is, now let's address why it exists.

WHY DOES THE CHURCH EXIST?

Some churches have forgotten why they exist and end up doing anything and everything except what they were created to do. I believe this is an important issue and one of the reasons why thousands of churches are dying and closing every year. Alvin Reid and Mark Liederbach say, "When the church loses, forgets, or fails to emphasize the missional thrust of its purpose . . . it is a move away from a movement mentality toward what we would describe as 'institutionalism.'"[12]

Churches need to take a hard look in the mirror and ask themselves some tough questions about why they exist, and then do it. I want to offer several reasons why I believe the church exists and is still relevant for today.

To Grow

The local church plays an important role in our spiritual growth and development as disciples and followers of Jesus Christ. Churches should not simply be concerned with growing numbers, but with growing members through discipleship. Pastor Mark Dever says, "I've come to see that relationship with a local congregation is central to individual discipleship. The church isn't an optional extra; it's the shape of your following Jesus."[13]

Spiritual growth and discipleship happen in a number of ways through the local church. However, one of the primary ways the church makes disciples is by providing a place for us to hear, learn, and study the Word of God within the context of Christian community under godly leadership. Many local churches offer classes, training, and small groups that help Christians learn and apply the Bible to everyday life. When I was a new believer, my local church helped me learn to read my Bible and encouraged me to pray and to share my faith with others.

Learning about God's Word within the context of the local church allows us to ask important questions, dialogue, and learn from other believers who have more wisdom and experience.

To Belong

Many people are looking for a place to belong. TV shows like *Survivor* and *Big Brother* reveal people's innate need and longing for community. The social media phenomenon of Facebook, Twitter, and MySpace also demonstrates this fact. Despite all this technology and media to make us more connected, people are more depressed and lonely than ever before because they are in search of community. God created us to be with others in community. Problem is, many people are looking in the wrong places—bars and coffee shops. Reformer Martin Luther said, "God has created man for fellowship, and not for solitariness."[14]

At its very essence Christianity is about vital relationships. First and foremost, it's about a relationship with God the Father, through Jesus Christ, the Son. Second, it's about growing together with other believers who daily walk with us in the church.

Disciples are made in community, not isolation. We must rediscover the power of biblical community if we are going to make and be disciples for Christ. Community is not separate from discipleship; rather it is the entry point to the discipleship journey. The church provides a place for believers to live together in Christian community to support and encourage one another in the faith (see Galatians 6:1-2; Hebrews 10:24-25).

To Go

The church should realize that we gather together, not to stay together, but to scatter. The church was not designed to stay in one place, but to go out into the world in mission. As God the Father sent Jesus, He also sends the church into our time and culture as missionaries to make disciples. The Scriptures call each of us to be missionaries to the world around us. The church is not an end in itself but a missionary movement that must always seek to fulfill the mission of God.

Fulfilling God's mission is not just something we support or do in other countries. The United States is actually the new mission field. Hunger and poverty are a serious epidemic, not only in other countries but here as well. Every day millions of people live in poverty in the shadow of our nation's great wealth. Most of our nation's poor are children and elderly. More than 1.5 million American children do not have a home.[15] In addition, drugs, domestic violence, and illiteracy are harsh realities for many people. Every one of them was created by God and should not be considered just a number or mere statistic.

We have a scriptural mandate to be missionaries to our cities and communities by sharing the love and compassion of Christ. Matthew 9:35-36 tells us that when Jesus went out into all the cities and villages, He saw that the multitudes were weary and He had compassion on them. He saw—and met—the needs of people. We will never be missionaries until we get outside of the four walls of our churches and begin to do the same. If we are going to make a difference, we must roll up our sleeves and join in the work of Jesus among the poor and disenfranchised of this world. Find the needs of your community and begin to fill them. Every Christian and every church can be on mission for God to reach their community for Christ.

REFLECT AND RESPOND

In conclusion, the church is the body of Christ, and to reject it is to reject Him. If you want to see differences in the church, they will begin with you. The local church is God's plan for impacting this world for Christ. I want to challenge you to join the revolution and become a part of a local church, if you are not already. If you are, get more involved. Pray for your church, its leaders, and its members. They are your spiritual family, so take some time to get to know them. Take some time to reflect on the nature and purpose of the church and its implications for Christians everywhere.

1. There are many different points of view when it comes to the church. What does the Bible tell us about the nature of the church?
2. How does the biblical nature of the church differ from a more modern understanding of the church?
3. How has this chapter challenged your preconceived ideas about the church?
4. Many churches have forgotten their original purpose for being here. Why does the church exist and what are the implications for a church that is not living out its original purpose?
5. What are the implications of the universal and local nature of the church for you and me?
6. What is your experience with the church? Without getting too personal, share a good and bad experience. How have you personally benefited from being a part of a local church?

CHAPTER 6

FORGIVENESS AND ETERNAL LIFE: It's Still Amazing Grace

Grace is but glory begun, and glory is but grace perfected.
JONATHAN EDWARDS

WHAT'S SO AMAZING about grace? *Grace* is a very common word in our culture. Perhaps it's a little too common. It's as ordinary as the nose on our face or the sound of our voice. However, few people understand or believe in the true meaning of grace. Grace is more than a person's name or giving someone a second chance.

Christianity is predominantly a religion of grace, and to be a Christian is to affirm the importance of God's grace. In fact, grace is what makes Christianity unique among other faiths. Author Philip Yancey tells this story of C. S. Lewis on grace:

During a British conference on comparative religions, experts from around the world debated what, if any, belief was unique to the Christian faith. They began eliminating possibilities. Incarnation? Other religions had different versions of gods appearing in human form. Resurrection? Again, other religions had accounts of return from death. The debate went on for some time until C. S. Lewis wandered into the room.

"What's the rumpus about?" he asked, and heard in reply that his colleagues were discussing Christianity's unique contribution among world religions. Lewis responded, "Oh, that's easy. It's grace." . . . Only Christianity dares to make God's love unconditional.[1]

So what exactly is *grace*? Jerry Bridges rightly describes grace as, "God's free and unmerited favor shown to guilty sinners who deserve only judgment. It is the love of God shown to the unlovely. It is God reaching downward to people who are in rebellion against Him."[2] Grace means that our relationship with God is free and not based upon good deeds or anything that we can do. It means we can never be good enough to earn God's love. We can do nothing to make God love us more than He already does.

In reality, the Christian faith is a life-changing experience of God's forgiving and redeeming grace. The Bible says, "For by grace you have been saved through faith, and that not of yourselves; it is the gift of God, not of works, lest anyone should boast" (Ephesians 2:8-9, NKJV). Salvation is all grace, from beginning to end. Salvation is the free work of grace through faith. It's not based on anything we can do. God's love is demonstrated in that He forgives and justifies poor, lost sinners.

The last section of the Apostles' Creed focuses on the forgiveness of sins and eternal life. Both of these great spiritual truths flow from God's amazing grace and love for His people. God's grace is the foundation of the Christian faith because salvation begins and ends with His love for humanity.

PROFILES: Meet John Newton (1725–1807)

John Newton was born in London on July 24, 1725, the son of a commander of a merchant ship that sailed the Mediterranean. At age eleven Newton went to sea with his father and began the life of a seaman. He had many challenges at sea and eventually became captain of his own ship, which was involved with the slave trade.

In 1748, Newton had a spiritual conversion while sailing back to England aboard a merchant ship. The vessel encountered a severe storm and almost sank. Newton awoke in the middle of the night and called out to God as the ship was filling with water. He later marked this experience as the beginning of his conversion to Christianity. As he sailed home, Newton began to pray and read the Bible.

Newton eventually left the slave trade and became an ordained minister in the Church of England, abolitionist, and beloved hymn writer. Among Newton's contributions is the hymn "Amazing Grace," which is still sung in thousands of churches throughout the world. "Amazing Grace" beautifully describes God's free grace in song.

Amazing grace! How sweet the sound
That saved a wretch like me!
I once was lost, but now am found;
Was blind, but now I see.

'Twas grace that taught my heart to fear,
And grace my fears relieved;
How precious did that grace appear,
The hour I first believed!

Thro' many dangers, toils and snares,
I have already come;
'Tis grace has brought me safe thus far,
And grace will lead me home.

IT ALL BEGINS WITH GOD

How does God change people's hearts from the inside out, from sinners to saints? Many Christians know God has changed their life, but they lack an understanding of how. As we grow in faith, it becomes more important to understand the dynamics of salvation so that we may understand the preciousness of God's grace. Even the great preacher Charles Spurgeon grew in understanding of his salvation experience:

> One week-night, when I was sitting in the house of God, I was not thinking much about the preacher's sermon, for I did not believe it. The thought struck me, *How did you come to be a Christian?* I sought the Lord. *But how did you come to seek the Lord?* The truth flashed across my mind in a moment—I should not have sought Him unless there had been some previous influence in my mind to *make me* seek Him. I prayed, thought I, but then I asked myself, *How came I to pray?* I was induced to pray by reading the Scriptures. How came I to read the Scriptures? I did read them, but what led me to do so? Then, in a moment, I saw that God was at the bottom of it all, and that He was the Author of my faith, and so the whole doctrine of grace opened up to me, and from that doctrine I have not departed to this day, and I desire to make this my constant confession, "I ascribe my change wholly to God."[3]

Think about your own salvation experience for a minute. Did you do anything to earn it? What happened in your life to bring you to the point of receiving Christ? Like Spurgeon, you will probably find that "God was at the bottom of it all."

When I was around the age of fifteen, I began experimenting with drugs and alcohol, and by my junior year in high school I almost dropped out of school. Things kept going from bad to worse. Around the age of nineteen, I began to search for the meaning of life and to question the existence of God. For the first time in my life I had a growing awareness of my own personal need for God. I began to feel that there had to be more to life than the way I was living, because the way I was living only brought me misery.

Then one day I felt compelled to go to the lake near my house to think about the meaning of life. Little did I know that this would be a crossroad experience in my life. While I was at the lake, sitting on a rock, I broke down in tears and told God I wanted to turn from my destructive ways. At that moment the peace of God flooded my soul and my sins were washed away. Sitting on a rock by the edge of the water, I accepted Jesus Christ into my heart as my Lord and Savior. I have been following Jesus since then, and I am still going strong after all these years.

My salvation experience had little to do with me or my own goodness. Like Spurgeon, I ascribe it wholly to God. Salvation always begins and ends with God: He is "the author and finisher of our faith" (Hebrews 12:2, NKJV). Just as a baby can't make itself be born, neither can we save ourselves. Only God's grace can save us. There is no other way. Personal salvation is God's work in us, through and through from beginning to end.

JUSTIFIED BY FAITH

Martin Luther was someone else who discovered the grace of God. He was born November 10, 1483, in Eisleben, Germany. After almost dying in a lightning storm, Luther joined the monastery of the Augustinian Order in Erfurt where strict discipline was expected and enforced. He gave himself completely to the rigorous monastic life of prayer, study, and the daily practice of the sacraments, and regularly confessed his sins to a priest. He was trying to earn his salvation through good works, but nothing would satisfy his inner longing for acceptance from God.

Luther became a full-time professor at the University of Wittenberg where he taught theology and Bible. There he began to study the books of Romans and Galatians. These two New Testament writings helped him discover the doctrine of justification by faith and salvation by grace.

After years of wrestling with God, Martin Luther finally accepted the grace of God. He beautifully described his personal experience of justification by faith in the following way:

> Night and day I pondered until I saw the connection between the justice of God and the statement that "the just shall live by his faith." Then I grasped that the justice of God is that righteousness by which through grace and sheer mercy God justifies us through faith. Thereupon I felt myself to be reborn and to have gone through open doors into paradise. The whole of Scripture took on a new meaning, and whereas before the "justice of God" had filled me with hate, now it became to me inexpressibly sweet in greater love.[4]

Luther radically opposed the unbiblical practices of the Catholic Church that undermined the grace of God. In 1517, he identified ninety-five practices of the church that he contested, calling his list the Ninety-Five Theses, and nailed it on the doors of the cathedral in Wittenberg. This act marked the beginning of the Protestant Reformation and the rediscovery of the doctrine of "justification by grace through faith alone."

What is *justification*? Justification is what God does for us. It is an unmerited act of God by which we are forgiven for our sins and brought into a right relationship with God through the work of Jesus Christ. Through justification God redeems all who put their faith in Christ alone for their salvation. Paul describes justification by faith in Romans 3:23-26:

> For all have sinned and fall short of the glory of God, and are justified by his grace as a gift, through the redemption that is in Christ Jesus, whom God put forward as a propitiation by his blood, to be received by faith. This was to show God's

righteousness, because in his divine forbearance he had passed over former sins. It was to show his righteousness at the present time, so that he might be just and the justifier of the one who has faith in Jesus.

This passage reveals two vital truths about justification. First, we all have sinned and need God's grace. Through justification by faith our status is changed from condemned sinner to justified child of God. Justification is the free gift of God's unmerited grace by which He forgives sinners and declares them righteous. Second, God freely justifies us by grace through faith in Jesus Christ. It is by the merits of Christ's redemptive work on the cross that we receive justification and the forgivness of sins. Paul makes it clear that justification comes by grace through faith in God alone not of works (see Romans 3:24; Ephesians 2:8-9). D. A. Carson warns us to never lose sight of the cross: "I fear that the cross, without ever being disowned, is constantly in danger of being dismissed from the central place it must enjoy, by relatively peripheral insights that take on far too much weight."[5] Let us never forget the price of Jesus' cross and the vital doctrine of justification.

GOING DEEPER: Five Solas of the Reformation

Five foundations summarized the theological reforms of the Reformation in the fifteenth and sixteen centuries. These banners were known as the Five Solas (sola is Latin, meaning "only" or "alone") of the Reformation and emphasized the authority of Scripture, salvation in Christ alone, by grace alone, through faith alone, and to God alone be glory.

In April 1996, the Alliance of Confessing Evangelicals drafted the Cambridge Declaration as a call to the evangelical church to recover the biblical doctrines of the Reformation. The Cambridge Declaration explains the importance of regaining adherence to the Five Solas of the Reformation.[6]

Here are the Five Solas:

1. **Sola Scriptura (Scripture alone).** We reaffirm the inerrant Scripture to be the sole source of written divine revelation, which alone can bind the conscience. The Bible alone teaches all that is necessary for our salvation from sin and is the standard by which all Christian behavior must be measured.
2. **Solus Christus (Christ alone).** We reaffirm that our salvation is accomplished by the mediatorial work of the historical Christ alone. His sinless life and substitutionary atonement alone are sufficient for our justification and reconciliation to the Father.
3. **Sola Gratia (Grace alone).** We reaffirm that in salvation we are rescued from God's wrath by his grace alone. It is the supernatural work of the Holy Spirit that brings us to Christ by releasing us from our bondage to sin and raising us from spiritual death to spiritual life.
4. **Sola Fide (Faith alone).** We reaffirm that justification is by grace alone through faith alone because of Christ alone. In justification Christ's righteousness is imputed to us as the only possible satisfaction of God's perfect justice.
5. **Soli Deo Gloria (Glory to God alone).** We reaffirm that because salvation is of God and has been accomplished by God, it is for God's glory and that we must glorify him always. We must live our entire lives before the face of God, under the authority of God and for his glory alone.

THE NEW CREATION

One of the greatest blessings and joys of my job as pastor is getting to see God change people's lives. It never gets old. Let me tell you about Big Dave. He is a former bouncer and Green Beret who rides a giant

Harley and trains men to work in counterterrorism in dangerous countries overseas. Some Christians have a saying that you should not drink, cuss, smoke, or chew or hang out with people who do. Well, Dave was one of those people. Throughout most of his life he partied hard and lived for the things of the world, but they never satisfied him. There was always something missing. As Dave found out, it was a relationship with God. One day, he found our church at a local surf report website, began attending, and became a believer.

Dave was a little rough at first, but now God is using him to reach military men whom you and I would never be able to reach. Over the years Dave and I have become great friends, and I have had the privilege of baptizing Dave in the ocean as well as officiating his wedding. Dave is a changed man and his story is one of the most dramatic and amazing stories of God's grace I have ever known. Most Christians would be afraid to even talk to a guy like Dave about their faith, but his life is changed, and God is using him today for His glory.

God still changes people today. The Bible calls the change that God produces in a person's life regeneration. *Regeneration* means a total transformation of heart and soul in which the new believer is literally made a new creature. Paul says, "If anyone is in Christ, he is a new creature; the old things passed away; behold, new things have come" (2 Corinthians 5:17, NASB).

Author Stephen Smallman uses the biblical analogy of physical birth to help people understand the process of regeneration in what he calls the spiritual birthline. He says, "I take the familiar process of physical birth—conception, pregnancy, delivery, and growth—as a means to understand the less familiar idea of spiritual birth."[7] The analogy of the new birth helps us understand the dynamic process of salvation and explains why new believers are like newborns. They need special love and attention because they have not yet learned the basics of their faith or the spiritual disciplines that help them grow.

Jesus discussed the new birth with Nicodemus in John 3:3-8:

Jesus answered him, "Truly, truly, I say to you, unless one is born again he cannot see the kingdom of God." Nicodemus said to him, "How can a man be born when he is old? Can he enter a second time into his mother's womb and be born?" Jesus answered, "Truly, truly, I say to you, unless one is born of water and the Spirit, he cannot enter the kingdom of God. That which is born of the flesh is flesh, and that which is born of the Spirit is spirit. Do not marvel that I said to you, 'You must be born again.' The wind blows where it wishes, and you hear its sound, but you do not know where it comes from or where it goes. So it is with everyone who is born of the Spirit."

Take a moment and think about how this analogy fits with your experience or others you know who are new believers.

GROWING IN GRACE

Regeneration is not the end. It is just the beginning of the journey of faith. Just as infants continue to grow and develop, so we continue to mature once we become believers. Spiritual growth is a major theme of the Bible. We are to grow in the grace and knowledge of God (see 2 Peter 3:18). While salvation happens in a moment, spiritual growth and discipleship is an ongoing process that never ends until we see Jesus face-to-face.

If we are going to continue to grow in our faith, we need to develop spiritual disciplines in our lives. Author Donald Whitney says, "Spiritual Disciplines are those personal and corporate disciplines that promote spiritual growth."[8] The spiritual disciplines promote spiritual growth and godliness, helping us to grow in godliness and become more like Jesus. According to the Bible, godliness and Christlikeness is the goal of the disciplines. Paul says to, "Discipline yourself for the purpose of godliness" (1 Timothy 4:7, NASB).

Discipline literally means "exercise." Therefore, spiritual disciplines are spiritual exercises. The word *discipline* comes from the Greek word *gumnasia,* which *gymnasium* comes from. Just as physical exercise promotes strength in the body, the spiritual disciplines promote godliness and growth in grace. Many of us are simply concerned with being physically fit through working out and dieting. What if we applied the same care and discipline to our spiritual fitness as we do to our physical fitness?

Here is a short list of spiritual disciplines from Donald Whitney's *Spiritual Disciplines for the Christian Life* that, if practiced regularly, can help you continue to grow in your faith.

- Bible Intake
- Prayer
- Worship
- Evangelism
- Serving
- Stewardship
- Fasting
- Silence and Solitude
- Journaling
- Learning

ETERNAL LIFE

Death is not the end of the journey. The hymn writer John Newton penned, "Tis grace has brought me safe thus far, and grace will lead me home." Heaven is our eternal home, and eternal life is the promise and culmination of our salvation in Jesus Christ. Life everlasting in which we will abide with God in heaven forever is the final destination of the journey of faith. Wayne Grudem describes it as "the final step in the application of redemption. It will happen when Christ returns and raises from the dead the bodies of all believers for all time who have died, and reunites them with their souls, and changes the bodies of all believers who remain alive, thereby giving all believers at the same time perfect resurrection bodies like his own."[9]

The Bible places an important emphasis on the hope of resurrection and eternal life through Christ (see 1 Corinthians 15:12-49; Philippians 3:21). Jesus declared, "I am the resurrection and the life. He who believes in Me, though he may die, he shall live. And whoever lives and believes in Me shall never die" (John 11:25-26, NKJV). Jesus invites us to experience the power of the Resurrection for ourselves. We can have hope for today, tomorrow, and eternity because of the Resurrection.

The Resurrection gives us hope of the future glory and grace that is promised to believers. It reminds us to keep our eyes on heaven and not on the things of this earth. Paul says, "The sufferings of this present time are not worthy to be compared with the glory which shall be revealed in us" (Romans 8:18, NKJV). Revelation 21:3-4 declares the promise of the future glory that is reserved for those who believe in Jesus Christ:

Behold, the tabernacle of God is with men, and He will dwell with them, and they shall be His people. God Himself will be with them and be their God. And God will wipe away every tear from their eyes; there shall be no more death, nor sorrow, nor crying. There shall be no more pain, for the former things have passed away. (NKJV)

REFLECT AND RESPOND

This section has been an introduction to the great truths that are in the Apostles' Creed. I know that I have only briefly touched on some of the great truths about salvation. It has been like scratching the tip of the iceberg. My hope and prayer is that you will not stop here, but that you will continue to go further and study these great truths for yourself.

I encourage you to take some time to stop and reflect on how truly amazing God's grace is. It's absolutely free and cannot be earned. Think about when you first responded to God's call and how you came to faith. Get a journal and write down your testimony and share it with others. What are the evidences of grace in your life today?

This is also a good time to stop and ask yourself, Am I really a follower of Christ? Has God changed my life and do I really believe that Jesus Christ is Lord? Do I have the assurance of salvation in my life? If you find in your heart that you are not a believer, all you need to do is put your faith and hope in Jesus as Lord and Savior. Confess your sins and simply trust in Him alone to save you through what He has done for you on the cross. Surrender your life to Him today, receive His saving grace, and begin to follow Him.

1. What is so amazing about grace? Discuss the concept of grace. Why is it unique to the Christian faith and message?

2. Reflect on Spurgeon's salvation story. What features of his experience stand out to you most?

3. What does it mean to be justified by faith? Why is this doctrine important for Christians to understand?

4. Regeneration refers to the change that God works in our heart and soul when we become believers. What is the biblical metaphor for regeneration?

5. From the moment we are "born again," we continue to grow until one day we join God in heaven. What are some of the ways that we continue to grow in our faith?

6. Death is not the end, but only the beginning of the next step in our relationship with God. What does it mean to receive eternal life and when does that happen?

PART 2

THE TEN COMMANDMENTS

The Ethical Foundation of the Christian Faith

THE TEN COMMANDMENTS are ten laws God wrote on tablets of stone at Mount Sinai for the prophet Moses to give to the children of Israel. These laws were to be used to govern the nation of Israel. This significant moment in Israel's history, recorded in Exodus 20:2-17 and Deuteronomy 5:6-21, has been depicted in numerous movies and storybooks. The Ten Commandments are also called the Decalogue, from the Greek term meaning "ten words."

The Ten Commandments reflect God's character and represent His universal moral law, which is a biblical standard of moral conduct for all of humanity. Not only are they historically significant, but they also offer guidance and wisdom for all time.

The Ten Commandments begin with God saying, "I am the LORD your God, who brought you out of the land of Egypt, out of the house of slavery" (Exodus 20:2). God then goes on to list the commandments:

1. "You shall have no other gods before me" (verse 3).
2. "You shall not make for yourself a carved image, or any likeness of anything that is in heaven above, or that is in the earth beneath, or that is in the water under the earth" (verse 4).
3. "You shall not take the name of the LORD your God in vain, for the LORD will not hold him guiltless who takes his name in vain" (verse 7).
4. "Remember the Sabbath day, to keep it holy" (verse 8).
5. "Honor your father and your mother, that your days may be long in the land that the LORD your God is giving you" (verse 12).
6. "You shall not murder" (verse 13).
7. "You shall not commit adultery" (verse 14).
8. "You shall not steal" (verse 15).
9. "You shall not bear false witness against your neighbor" (verse 16).
10. "You shall not covet your neighbor's house; you shall not covet your neighbor's wife, or his male servant, or his female servant, or his ox, or his donkey, or anything that is your neighbor's" (verse 17).

CHAPTER 7

WHATEVER HAPPENED TO MORALITY?

The Moral Law tells us the tune we have to play: our instincts are merely the keys.

C. S. LEWIS

ONE OF MY earliest memories is from a day when I was playing on the staircase of my childhood home. I can still remember the blue 1970s shag carpet that covered the steps. But what makes that day stand out so vividly in my memory is that is was the first time I lied to my mother. I have long since forgotten the lie, but I will never forget the strange, awkward feeling in my stomach that came as a result of knowing I had done something wrong.

How did I know that lying was wrong? Or, for that matter, how does anyone know when he or she has done something wrong? Where does our sense of right and wrong come from? It is by God's moral law, which is universal to every living human being. God's moral law is within every one of us. I want to take the next few pages to unpack the importance of knowing and understanding the moral law today.

THE LAY OF THE LAW

Have you noticed that no one talks about ethics or morality anymore? Even in churches it's rare to hear about the moral law. Research shows that less than 60 percent of Americans even know five of the Ten Commandments. Researcher George Barna says, "No wonder people break the Ten Commandments all the time. They don't know what they are. . . . Increasingly, America is biblically illiterate."[1]

You might recall the crude and obnoxious cartoon called *Beavis and Butt-head*. Beavis and Butt-head were two slacker teens who played video games, listened to heavy metal, and liked to burn and destroy things. Many people in my generation were inspired to be rebellious because of this television show. One of their favorite taglines was, "Breaking the law, breaking the law." These two teens, who both gloried in rebelling and breaking the law, were radical examples of human nature. We all are lawbreakers from birth.

So what is the law? To answer that question we must look at the three different types of laws in the Bible: judicial law, ritual law, and moral law.

Judicial law. The political and judicial laws of the Old Testament were given specifically to Israel to govern civil and social life and to bring stability. Judicial laws enforced such penalties as stoning, "an eye for an eye," and other harsh practices that are no longer binding because we don't live in a theocracy under the rule of God.

Ritual law. The Jewish scribes and Pharisees practiced ritual laws, which were ceremonial, dietary, and sacrificial. The religious leaders developed ritual laws for just about everything you can imagine, and eventually they numbered in the hundreds. These laws included things like ceremonial cleansing, not eating certain foods, and observing religious days. We can be thankful that the coming of Jesus cancelled out these laws (see Matthew 15:20; Mark 7:15-19).

Moral law. The Ten Commandments contain God's moral law and ethical standards for Christian living. They also reflect His holiness and reveal His standard of moral conduct for all of humanity. These laws are still binding for all people.

The moral law has several important functions:

1. It is a mirror that reveals God's perfect holiness and our sinfulness.
2. It reflects our sin, shortcomings, and inability to live up to God's perfection.
3. It reminds us of our need for God's grace and mercy and our personal need for a Savior.

As believers, we are to look to the law as a guide for moral conduct, not as a means of earning our salvation.

PROFILES: Meet John Calvin (1509–1564)

Born July 10, 1509, in the town of Noyon in Picardy, near Paris, France, John Calvin grew up to become a theological giant. He studied law and eventually earned his doctorate in law. In 1531, he converted from Catholicism to Protestantism. In March 1536, Calvin published the first edition of his *Institutes of the Christian Religion*, which became one of the most important documents of faith for the Protestant Reformation.

Through God's providence, Calvin ended up in Geneva, where he became one of the dominant leaders of the Reformation movement. During his ministry in Geneva, Calvin preached over two thousand sermons. On average, he preached twice on Sunday and three times during the week. His sermons, which were delivered without notes, directly from the Hebrew or the Greek, usually lasted more than an hour.

Calvin and other Reformers believed that the moral law has three uses—it reveals and condemns sin, it points sinners to Christ, and it provides a guide for the Christian life. Here is Calvin on the third use of the law:

> *Only if we walk in the beauty of God's law do we become sure of our adoption as children of the Father. The Law of God contains in itself the dynamic of the new life by which his image is fully restored in us; but by nature we are sluggish, and therefore, we need to be stimulated, aided in our efforts by a guiding principle. . . . The plan of Scripture for a Christian walk is twofold: first, that we be instructed in the law to love righteousness, because by nature we are not inclined to do so; second, that we be shown a simple rule that we may not waver in our race.*[2]

JESUS AND THE LAW

Jesus came, not to do away with the law, but to fulfill it and set us free from the law as a system of salvation (see Matthew 5:17; Romans 6:14; 7:4,6; 1 Corinthians 9:20; Galatians 2:15-19; 3:25). He fulfilled the law by becoming the Lamb of God. In the Jewish sacrificial system, the priest would sacrifice a Passover lamb in the temple to atone for the people's sins. The blood was sprinkled on the altar and the whole lamb was eaten. In the original Passover in Egypt, the blood was smeared on the doorposts of each household (see Exodus 12:1-28).

Christians believe that the suffering servant of Isaiah 53 refers to Jesus Christ. According to Isaiah 53, the suffering servant is "like a lamb that is led to the slaughter" (verse 7) and "his soul makes an offering for guilt" (verse 10).

Jesus became the atonement that replaced the sacrificial lambs, whose blood was necessary for the forgiveness of sins in the Jewish sacrificial system. By becoming the sacrificial Lamb of God, Jesus fulfilled the law, which enabled Him to offer forgiveness of our sins and to set us free from the power of sin and death forever. Christ is the end of the law (see Romans 10:4). Hebrews 10:10 says, "We have been made holy through the sacrifice of the body of Jesus Christ once for all" (NIV).

DELIGHTING IN THE LAW

At first glance the law and commandments may seem a little overwhelming and even legalistic. However, Jesus summarized the commandments by saying, "'Love the Lord your God with all your heart and with all your soul and with all your mind.' This is the first and greatest commandment. And the second is like it: 'Love your neighbor as yourself.' All the Law and the Prophets hang on these two commandments" (Matthew 22:36-40, NIV).

According to Jesus, the law and the commandments are all about love; indeed, the law begins with God's love for us. The preface of the Ten Commandments reminds Israel that God is their Savior: "I am the LORD your God, who brought you out of Egypt, out of the house of slavery" (Exodus 20:2). Christian love finds its source from God alone, because God is love. Love is not what He does, but who He is because God's very essence is love. Love flows from Him to all His creation. John reminds us, "This is love: not that we loved God, but that he loved us and sent his Son as an atoning sacrifice for our sins" (1 John 4:10, NIV). Love begins and ends with God.

It's not legalism to keep God's law; it's walking in love. Paul says, "The goal of this command is love, which comes from a pure heart and a good conscience and a sincere faith" (1 Timothy 1:5, NIV). Because of God's love for us, we should love Him and others, and keep His commandments: "The whole law is fulfilled in one word: 'You shall love your neighbor as yourself'" (Galatians 5:14).

We can respond to God's love for us by living out the commandments. Many of the Reformers had a positive view of the law for this very reason. In the Reformed tradition, the Heidelberg Catechism included the law under the heading of Gratitude because we should be grateful to God for delivering and saving us. Delighting in and keeping the law is our way of showing our gratitude and thanks to God for loving us and for saving us from our sins.

THE TEN COMMANDMENTS

The Ten Commandments can be divided into two categories: love for God and love for our neighbors. The first four commandments deal with how to love and reverence God, and they help us understand our moral responsibility toward Him. The final six commandments tell us how to love our neighbors and establish boundaries for how we are to treat others. Keep this in mind as we look at each of the Ten Commandments.

1. The Main Thing: Have No Other Gods

The first commandment reminds us to keep the main thing the main thing: "Have no other gods before me" (Exodus 20:3). Everything begins and ends with God. He always comes first, and so the first two commandments are about honoring and worshipping Him, the one true God. They affirm that there is only one God and remind us that we should put no other gods before Him. As God's people, we should honor, worship, and show reverence toward Him because He has redeemed and delivered us from our sin.

The Israelites were surrounded by nations who believed in many gods (polytheism). In contrast, the Jews worshipped the one true God (monotheism). Their unique commitment to God distinguished them from the other nations. In the same way, Christians believe in one God who is sovereign over all things. Let's keep God the main thing in our lives. As Jesus said, "Seek first the kingdom of God and his righteousness" (Matthew 6:33).

2. Be Careful What You Worship:
Don't Make Carved Images

The second commandment is a reminder to not worship anything but God. Within every one of us is the innate desire to worship because God created us to worship Him—Him alone. The ancient pagans created false idols carved from wood and other earthen materials to worship as their gods. Instead of worshipping the one true God, they chose to worship gods made with their own hands.

The book of Exodus tells us that the Israelites created a golden calf to worship, even after God delivered them from the bondage of Egypt (see Exodus 32). If God is not the center of our lives, we will worship other gods. John Calvin rightly said, "Our hearts are an idol factory." What is an idol? Pastor Timothy Keller says, "It is anything more important to you than God, anything that absorbs your heart and imagination more than God, anything you seek to give you what only God can give."[3] Anything can become an idol. Today, many people have personal idols and worship things such as money, cars, boats, and even celebrities. God alone is worthy of our worship. We must continually ask ourselves, Who or what do I worship?

3. Don't Misuse It: Don't Take the Lord's Name in Vain

As we discussed in chapter 3, names are very important. God's name was a gift of grace to the people of Israel. God was not worshipped through an idol or carved image, but through His name. God's name is holy and not to be taken lightly. The Jewish people reverenced the name of the Lord so much that they would not even spell it out, or use it publically. Taking God's name in vain includes cursing, swearing, lying, or using it in any disrespectful way. We should use His name only with respect and reverence, especially in prayer and worship.

God's name has power, and it is to be reverenced. When teaching the disciples how to pray, Jesus said we are to begin praying by saying, "Hallowed be your name" (Matthew 6:9). Numerous New Testament references talk about praying in the name of Jesus. Jesus Himself said,

"Most assuredly, I say to you, whatever you ask the Father in My name He will give you" (John 16:23, NKJV). When we pray in Jesus' name, God the Father hears us and responds. God's name reminds us to rely on Him as our source of power and strength.

4. A Day to Remember: Keep the Sabbath Holy

People are busier than ever before. With all of our technology and media, who has time to rest? If we are not careful, we will experience spiritual burnout. Spiritual burnout occurs when we don't give ourselves time to rest from our daily routine.

One of God's greatest gifts to humankind is the Sabbath, and we modern-day Christians need to step back and relearn God's principle of Sabbath rest. Our souls need spiritual rest in the same way that our physical bodies need rest. God commanded us to keep the Sabbath so that we might get the rest we need.

Throughout the Bible, God promises rest to His people. The biblical word for *rest* literally means "a resting place, a quiet place, peace, trust, and reliance." We need to allow time during each day for spiritual rest and solitude from all of the busy distractions of our complex world.

In the Bible the Sabbath also refers to a specific day of rest for worship. The Jews observed the Sabbath on Saturday, but for various reasons, Christians moved their day of worship to Sunday, which we continue to practice today. A Sabbath is not meant to be a burden, but a blessing from our work. God appointed a day and time for us to rest, worship, and hear the preaching of the Word. I encourage you to take time to turn off your phone, computer, and TV and find a day of Sabbath rest every week.

God has given His children a great gift in the Sabbath. I've learned to keep a Sabbath, and it has been one of the greatest spiritual discoveries I have found in the past few years. I went through a season of life where I became obsessed with my work and I nearly burned myself out. Recently, I have begun to take a Sabbath day off and it's been amazing!

On Saturdays our family spends the entire day together, and we have begun to grow together as a family. Also, since I am a pastor, I take every Monday off from my work to read, write, and reflect on what God is doing in my life.

5. Family Matters: Honor Your Father and Your Mother

The final six commandments toward loving others begin with the fifth commandment to honor your father and your mother. The family matters to God—it is God's first institution and should be a place where parents and children love, honor, and respect each other. This commandment is specifically directed toward children to honor and respect their parents. This is relevant for children of all ages, both young and old. Young children should obey and submit to their parents, and even adults should still show honor to their parents long after they have left the home and the discipline of their parents.[4] In the ancient Jewish culture believers thought that being disrespectful to your parent was a serious issue and showed disrespect for the Lord.[5]

It is important to say that this commandment presupposes that parents are doing their duty to support, encourage, and love their kids. The Bible tells parents, "Train up a child in the way he should go; even when he is old he will not depart from it" (Proverbs 22:6). Whether in the mall or the grocery store, we all have seen kids who are disrespectful and not submissive to their parents, obviously needing to be disciplined. Many times this is the result of a lack of parenting. Parents should discipline their children and set boundaries for them.[6] If parents will not discipline their children, who will? I think one of the major problems in our society is that many parents are not involved in their children's lives and basically let children raise themselves. Is it any wonder that children are so disrespectful toward adults in general and their parents in specific?

Lastly, I want to say that it's impossible for children to honor and obey their parents if their parents are abusive, behaving sinfully, or simply neglecting their children. It is the spiritual responsibility of parents to nurture, love, and teach their children about the faith. I am the father of two small girls whom I deeply love. I can only expect them to honor me if I am fulfilling my role as a godly father by loving them and training them in the faith.

6. The Sanctity of Life: You Shall Not Murder

Every human life has value and is sacred because every person is uniquely created in the image of God. Not only should we strive to not harm others, but we should also seek what is best for others. We should always value the sanctity of human life because every person belongs to God.

One of my favorite books and movies of all time is *The Lord of the Rings.* The main character is a small hobbit named Frodo who sets out with several other companions to destroy the ring of power. In discussing the corrupt and twisted creature named Gollum, who wants to take the ring for himself, Frodo says to his friend Gandalf the wizard, "It's a pity Bilbo didn't kill him when he had the chance." Gandalf replies, "Pity? It was pity that stayed Bilbo's hand. Many that live deserve death, and some that die deserve life. Can you give it to them, Frodo? Do not be too eager to deal out death in judgment . . . even the very wise cannot see all ends. My heart tells me that Gollum has some part to play yet, for good or ill, before this is over. The pity of Bilbo may rule the fate of many."[7] This story reminds us of the importance of human life, even for the worst individuals.

Jesus takes this commandment a step further by saying, "You have heard that the ancients were told, 'YOU SHALL NOT COMMIT MURDER' and 'Whoever commits murder shall be liable to the court.' But I say to you everyone who is angry with his brother shall be guilty before the court" (Matthew 5:21-22, NASB). Jesus is warning us about committing murder in our heart because the heart is the place where evil thoughts originate. When we let anger fester and build up, we are in a dangerous place with God. Take some time to examine your heart today and see if you are holding any anger toward others.

7. A Heart Check: You Shall Not Commit Adultery

The seventh commandment is meant to protect the sacredness of marriage. Marriage is an exclusive relationship between one man and one woman who have committed themselves together in the covenant of marriage.

Committing to a spouse isn't supposed to be like leasing a car—returning it whenever you're done. Yet nearly 50 percent of all marriages in North America end in divorce. The statistics prove that the sacredness of marriage is in trouble.

Both husbands and wives have an important role to play in making a marriage healthy and whole. Spouses should love, honor, and be faithful to each other in every way—spiritually, emotionally, and physically. Fidelity to a spouse begins in the heart. Every one of us should lead a pure life, free from lust and sexual immorality. Jesus said, "Everyone who looks at a woman with lustful intent has already committed adultery with her in his heart" (Matthew 5:28). According to Jesus, we can commit adultery in our hearts and minds just as if it was the actual sexual sin. It is important to guard our hearts from pornography, media, and other things that may lead us into sexual sin.

8. Everything Belongs to God: You Shall Not Steal

God has given each of us the right to own private property and possessions, and it should go without saying that we should not take money, possessions, or property that belongs to someone else. Instead, we should help to improve and protect the possessions of others. Ultimately, everything belongs to God, and to steal from others in a sense is to steal from Him. We need to be content with what we have and get our eyes off of what we don't have.

Most of us probably don't have a problem with intentionally stealing things from others, but what about taking things that don't technically belong to you, such as office supplies that include pens and paper? Or what about borrowing something with the intent of not returning it? (As I write this, I am reminded of something that I need to return to a friend.)

So why do people steal anyway? I think it has little to do with money. It comes from a longing deep within to selfishly possess things that do not belong to us. Some people steal just for the fun of it, while other people steal because it is a symptom of other sinful behavior, such as sloth, jealousy, and covetousness. Regardless of the motivation, stealing is always wrong.

9. Speak the Truth: Don't Bear False Witness

We are to always speak the truth, even if it hurts us or doesn't get us ahead. In the original context, this commandment refers to lying against our neighbor in court. However, we should be honest in our public and private dealings with others, regardless of the outcome or reason. We should always tell the truth, no matter what the cost.

Throughout the Bible God warns us against deception in any form. In our culture, some people think it is acceptable to tell little white lies. However, all lies are the same in God's eyes. Lying is never acceptable in any way, shape, or form. God is the Author of truth and as Christians we are to always walk in the truth.

10. Be Content: You Shall Not Covet

The final commandment is probably the hardest because it is one that only God can know or see. To covet is to desire something that belongs to another, which goes beyond simply admiring someone else's possessions. We should not desire or covet our neighbor's house, spouse, television sets, stereos, cars . . . the list could go on and on. Coveting can be sinister and includes envying, jealousy, stealing, and even murder.

The Rolling Stones wrote a song called, "You Can't Always Get What You Want." The next line reminds us that we get what we need. In a way, this is what Christianity represents. God provides for our needs, but not necessarily our wants. We should strive to be content with what we have, and be happy for others who have more than we do, or who have things we don't. It's possible to appreciate what others have without coveting those things. When we decide to be content with what God has given us, we experience freedom.

REFLECT AND RESPOND

The commandments remind us that God is not only concerned with our relationship with Him, but also our relationship with others. In fact, how we treat others is a direct reflection of our relationship with God. The Bible says, "A new commandment I give to you, that you love one another: just as I have loved you, you also are to love one another. By this all people will know that you are my disciples, if you have love for one another" (John 13:34-35). Our love for others is one of the distinguishing marks of authentic Christianity.

Going through these commandments, I can't help but think how straightforward and universal they are. They are so simple, yet we break them all the time. When was the last time you broke the Sabbath, took the Lord's name in vain, or wanted something that belonged to someone else?

The ultimate point of the moral law isn't condemnation, but liberation. It reminds us of our need for God's gospel of grace and mercy. It also reminds us of our responsibility toward others. Take a few minutes to think about the weight of your own sinfulness and the greatness of God's grace. How often do you take others into consideration before you act or make decisions?

1. What is God's moral law? How is it universally binding upon all people?
2. Can we expect everyone to live according to the Ten Commandments even if they are not true believers? Explain your answer.

3. Did you know the Ten Commandments before this study? Do your best to recite them now.

4. Why did God originally give the Ten Commandments to Moses and the children of Israel? What is their significance for today?

5. Which one of the commandments challenges you the most? Explain.

6. Explain what Jesus taught about the law. How did He summarize it?

7. Which one of the Ten Commandments do you think Americans struggle with the most? Which one do you think most Christians struggle with?

PART 3

THE LORD'S PRAYER

*The Spiritual Foundation
of the Christian Faith*

THE LORD'S PRAYER, also known as the Our Father or Pater Noster, is the most universally and best-known Christian prayer of all time. It is read at funerals, weddings, and church services throughout the Christian world. Two versions of it occur in the New Testament, one in Matthew 6:9-13 and the other in Luke 11:2-4. The Lord's Prayer is the heart of Jesus' teaching on prayer and offers us an outline by which we can shape our own personal prayer life and learn to pray according to His will.

> Our Father in heaven,
> Hallowed be Your name.
> Your kingdome come.
> Your will be done
> On earth as it is in heaven.
> Give us this day our daily bread.
> And forgive us our debts,
> As we forgive our debtors.

And do not lead us into temptation,
But deliver us from the evil one.
For Yours is the kingdom and the
power and the glory forever. Amen. (Matthew 6:9-13, NKJV)

CHAPTER 8

LEARNING TO PRAY LIKE JESUS

Prayer can never be in excess.
C. H. SPURGEON

PRAYER IS LIKE a long journey that begins with the first step. Just as a baby learns how to walk with tiny steps, or a child learns how to ride a bicycle with training wheels, so we learn to pray by praying. There is no magic to it, we just pray.

As I think back on my prayers as a new believer in 1993, they seem childish and innocent. I didn't have my theology or life all together, but I loved God with all my heart—and God knew my heart. I have learned a couple of things along the way as I have grown in my faith. At times I thought I had it figured out and at other times I realized how little I actually knew about prayer. So I humbly write this chapter, not as one who has it all figured out, but as one who is still on the journey, trying to learn what prayer is all about.

PRAY LIKE JESUS

Prayer is like one of those abstract psychological tests that mean something different to everyone you show it to. Just ask some random people on the street what they think about prayer, and you'll see what I mean. Some think that prayer is a moment of silence and meditation. Others believe prayer is a formal ritual or something you do out of a sense of duty. Still others think prayer is a waste of time, because no one hears you anyway.

Some books on prayer may be helpful, but I believe many are not. The best place to go to find real answers to the questions of prayer is the Bible. It gives us the keys we need to develop a powerful prayer life. The Scriptures are full of examples of men and women who walked with God and used prayer to impact their world, and we can do the same thing through prayer. Most of all, I think we should look at Jesus' life and teaching on prayer if we are going to learn how to pray.

The disciples walked with Jesus for three years and saw Him perform many miracles. I think they were profoundly impacted by the example of His prayer life because they asked Jesus, "Lord, teach us to pray" (Luke 11:1). They could have asked Him anything in the world, but they chose to ask Him about prayer. They knew He had a powerful prayer life and deep devotion to His heavenly Father.

Prayer wasn't just a message that Jesus preached, it was the life He lived. In between preaching to thousands of people, performing miracles, feeding multitudes, and healing the sick, Jesus still managed to find time to pray in secret. Let's look at some of the Scriptures that tell us this:

- "He went up on the mountain by himself to pray. When evening came, he was there alone" (Matthew 14:23).
- "He departed and went into a desolate place" (Luke 4:42).
- "So He Himself often withdrew into the wilderness and prayed" (Luke 5:16, NKJV).
- "He went out to the mountain to pray, and continued all night in prayer" (Luke 6:12, NKJV).
- "[He] went up on the mountain to pray" (Luke 9:28).
- "He went out and departed to a solitary place; and there He prayed" (Mark 1:35, NKJV).

Jesus prayed at every major event in His life: His baptism (see Luke 3:21); the choice of apostles (see 6:12-13); His transfiguration (see 9:29); before the cross at Gethsemane (see 22:39-40); and on the cross (see 23:46). Even now He continues in prayer for us: "He always lives to make intercession for them" (Hebrews 7:25). Jesus sets the example of prayer for us to follow. The secret to His powerful prayer life is found in the Lord's Prayer. Despite how well known this prayer is, few people grasp the meaning. It is Jesus' definitive teaching on prayer. It is an outline by which we can shape our own personal prayer life and learn how to pray according to His will.

PROFILES: Meet Andrew Murray (May 9, 1828–January 18, 1917)

Andrew Murray was a writer, teacher, pastor, and noted missionary leader. He was born in Cape Town, South Africa, and his father was a Scottish Presbyterian serving the Dutch Reformed Church of South Africa. Andrew was educated at Aberdeen University, Scotland, and at Utrecht University in the Netherlands. He was ordained in 1848 and served in several churches throughout his lifetime. He was a major promoter of missions throughout South Africa.

Murray is best known for his devotional writings. Several of his books have become devotional classics. Among these are *Abide in Christ*, *Absolute Surrender*, *With Christ in the School of Prayer*, *The Spirit of Christ*, and *Waiting on God*. The majority of his writing was on prayer. He said of the Lord's Prayer:

> *While we ordinarily first bring our own needs to God in prayer, and then think of what belongs to God and his interests, the Master reverses the order. First Thy name, Thy kingdom, Thy will; then give us, forgive us, lead us, deliver us. . . . In true worship the Father must be first, must be all.*[1]

NOBODY LIKES A HYPOCRITE

Jesus begins His teaching on prayer by telling us how not to pray. Learning how not to do something is almost as important as learning how to do it. He said, "When you pray, you must not be like the hypocrites" (Matthew 6:5). Nobody likes a hypocrite, especially God. A hypocrite is a person who is a fake, and puts on a religious front and tries to seem spiritual when in fact he really is not. A Christian hypocrite is a person who acts super-spiritual and puts on a show for others to see. I can't think of anything worse than a hypocrite. Hypocrites have turned more people off to the Christian faith and message than anything else I know.

The big issue Jesus is addressing here is the motivation of prayer. He says the hypocrites love to pray on the street corners so that others can see them. Are we praying to be heard by God, or seen by people? When we pray, it needs to be for an audience of one. Our motivation in prayer needs to be God alone. So when we pray, Jesus tells us to go to a secret place and pray to our Father. He promises that if we pray in secret, He will reward us openly (see Matthew 6:6).

The Lord hears the prayers of a humble heart. One of my favorite parables about prayer is in Luke 18:9-14, where the Pharisee and tax collector come before God to pray. The Pharisee was proud and boastful, while the tax collector was humble and simply asked, "God, be merciful to me, a sinner!" (verse 13). Jesus tells us that those who exalt themselves will be humbled, and those who humble themselves will be exalted (see Luke 18:13-14). God hears the prayers of the humble, and if we humble ourselves in God's sight, He will hear us.

DON'T REPEAT YOURSELF

When we pray, we are not to keep repeating ourselves. We have all heard people who say the same thing over and over and pray as loud as they can. Don't do this! It's annoying to others and, besides, God is not deaf. He already knows what you need, even before you pray (see

Matthew 6:8), so you don't need to repeat yourself when talking with God in prayer.

Vain repetition reveals a lack of faith that God hears us when we pray. We repeat things over and over to people who we don't think are listening to us. Sometimes, in the mornings, I have to ask my six-year-old daughter several times to get out of bed before she hears me. God is not a six-year-old. We need to have faith that the Lord will hear our prayers. "Without faith it is impossible to please Him, for he who comes to God must believe that He is and that He is a rewarder of those who seek Him" (Hebrews 11:6, NASB). You cannot pray unless you have faith that God is able to hear you. So, when you pray, have faith and know that God hears your prayers and will answer you.

OUR FATHER IN HEAVEN

Many people think that prayer is about them; however, the Lord's Prayer begins with acknowledging God as our heavenly Father. Prayer begins with God, His kingdom, and His ways. So true prayer is putting God first and seeking first the kingdom and His will for our lives. Everything else flows from this foundation.

Knowing that God is our heavenly Father affects how we pray. We are not praying to some abstract being in outer space, but to our heavenly Father. Think about that for a minute. We previously discussed the importance of understanding the fatherhood of God, but the Lord's Prayer helps us apply the doctrine personally through prayer. It reminds us of who He is and who we are: God is our heavenly Father and we are His children. As our Father, He loves us and wants to take care of us, and we can come to Him in prayer.

MAKE HIS NAME HOLY

The second line of the Lord's Prayer is "Hallowed be Your name." To *hallow* means "to make holy." When we pray, we should glorify God's name through praise and worship. Prayer is an act of divine worship that begins by acknowledging God for who He is and praising Him for His mighty acts and greatness. Worship takes our eyes off of ourselves and puts our focus back onto God and His kingdom. When we begin our prayer by offering worship to God, it helps us keep the proper perspective on prayer.

HIS KINGDOM AND HIS WILL

The purpose of our prayer should be to pray for God's kingdom to come and His will to be done. While in the Garden of Gethsemane, Jesus told the Father, "Not my will, but yours, be done" (Luke 22:42). Prayer is not just coming to God with our own personal agenda; rather it is seeking His agenda for our lives. His ways are greater than our ways and His plan is always better than our plans.

Prayer is asking for God's will. God is not Santa Claus; He does not give us everything we ask for, or everything we want. The reason is simple: He knows what we need, not just what we want. We should distinguish between these two things as well. Many times the things we want are not what we need, and the things we need are not what we want. One reason we need to seek God's will is that our Father knows what is best for us. This is why the Lord's Prayer says, "Your will be done on earth as it is in heaven" (Matthew 6:10, NKJV). His will must always come before our will.

One of the best ways to pray for God's will is to pray according to the Scriptures. John 15:7 says, "If you abide in Me, and My words abide in you, you will ask what you desire, and it shall be done for you" (NKJV). If God's Word is in us, then His desires become our desires, and we can have the assurance that He hears our prayers. Make sure that your prayers are in line with Scripture, because the Lord always honors His Word. One way to pray according to the Scriptures is to use the book of Psalms, or the Lord's Prayer, as prayers. You can also pray Paul's prayers.[2]

HIS PROVISION

An important part of prayer is asking God to meet your needs: "Give us this day our daily bread" (Matthew 6:11, NKJV). We should not be afraid to ask the Lord to meet our needs because, in doing so, we acknowledge that He is Lord over our lives, and that everything we are and everything we have come from Him. Jesus isn't talking about praying for cars and material things, He's talking about asking God to provide our basic needs.

This prayer should help us overcome our anxieties about life and the future because God is in control. Many people live in fear of what the future may hold. As Christians we shouldn't live this way. Jesus said, "Do not worry about your life, what you will eat or drink; or about your body, what you will wear . . . your heavenly Father knows that you need them" (Matthew 6:25,32, NIV). We need to remind ourselves that God desires to take care of His children. Don't be afraid to ask; remember that God is your Father.

HIS FORGIVENESS

No one is perfect. We are broken, fallen, sinful people who desperately need the forgiveness of God. I need God's grace and forgiveness every day. Some days I need it more than others. I suspect it's the same for you.

The Lord's Prayer reminds us that we are able to come before a holy and just God, confess our sins, and receive forgiveness. Confession and forgiveness is cleansing: "He is faithful and just to forgive us our sins and to cleanse us from all unrighteousness" (1 John 1:9). Forgiveness isn't just for the lost, but for Christians, too.

Not only do we need to receive forgiveness for ourselves, but we need to give it away too. We should freely forgive others as God has freely forgiven us. Jesus gives significant attention to this truth: "For if you forgive men their trespasses, your heavenly Father will also forgive you. But if you do not forgive men their trespasses, neither will your Father forgive your trespasses" (Matthew 6:14-15, NKJV). God wants to bring healing and restoration to broken relationships. Earlier, Jesus warns us that if we have something against another person, we need to seek reconciliation (see 5:21-26).

HIS PROTECTION

Temptation and spiritual warfare are everyday realities of the Christian life. That's why we need God's help to protect us and give us strength to face these battles. Every day brings with it new challenges and new battles, but the good news is that God is with us. He is not absent or disengaged, but "an ever-present help in trouble" (Psalm 46:1, NIV).

We are in the midst of a spiritual battle and our "adversary the devil walks about like a roaring lion, seeking whom he may devour" (1 Peter 5:8, NKJV). Paul says, "We do not wrestle against flesh and blood, but against principalities, against powers, against the rulers of the darkness of this age, against spiritual hosts of wickedness in the heavenly places" (Ephesians 6:12, NKJV). Are you facing temptations, struggles, battles from within or the outside? Don't grow weary or give up. Allow the Lord to help you pray for victory in every area of your life.

HIS POWER

The Lord's Prayer ends in a doxology and praise to God and a call for us to savor God's kingdom and His glory: "For Yours is the kingdom and the power and the glory forever. Amen." We are so consumed with our plans and busy lives; we no longer live in amazement of God's splendor and greatness. The Bible tells us to "be still, and know that I am God" (Psalm 46:10). We need to stop and take time to reflect on God's greatness in our lives. When we glorify God, we experience great joy.

The Outer Banks is a beautiful stretch of islands on the coast of North Carolina. We have some of the most beautiful sunrises and sunsets, yet I usually don't take the time to stop and watch the sunsets.

However, recently, I pulled my car over to marvel at God's glory and to watch the red sun go down into the ocean. Tears came to my eyes as I thought about God's greatness. When was the last time you took a moment to pause and reflect on God's greatness? Take time this week to stop and glorify your God.

GOING DEEPER: Before You Pray

Before praying, take these six things into consideration.

1. **Schedule a regular prayer time.** Find a time every day to spend in prayer—and be consistent. This is important. Give yourself enough time to actually pray. Many people spend only a few minutes each day in prayer. Few people spend quality time in prayer. It takes time to drown out the cares of the world, sit and pray, and then allow God to speak to us.

2. **Find a quiet place to pray.** In a world full of distractions, we need a quiet place where we can allow God to speak to us in prayer. The most effective place to pray is in your quiet place. It could be anywhere, as long as it is private. You can use your garage, pantry, front porch, or any other creative place where you can get alone with God. Some people pray while driving in a car, others pray while working out or running.

3. **Try to limit distractions.** Don't pray in the same room that you may watch television or be tempted by other activities.

4. **Choose a Scripture to help you pray.** Prayerfully select a passage of Scripture that means something to you. Let it either focus on the goodness of God, the promises of God, or the worship of God.

5. **Allow time for God to speak to you.** This is the hardest part. Many people never hear the Lord speak to them simply because they don't allow Him to. We need to allow

time to sit and listen for God's voice. This was the difference between Eli and Samuel (see 1 Samuel 3). Samuel was open to hearing from the Lord. He said, "Speak, for your servant hears" (verse 10).

6. **Have a prayer list to guide your prayers.** Pray for your family, friends, church, and so on. This will ensure that you don't forget important things to pray for.

REFLECT AND RESPOND

Like so many others, you may be struggling with the whole prayer thing. Maybe you have tried to pray, but fall asleep after a few minutes. Or maybe you get distracted whenever you pray and find your mind wandering. Don't give up if you're just starting to learn how to pray or having trouble praying. Hang in there, persevere, and press on. Throughout the Bible there are stories of men and women who persevered in prayer. Luke 18:1-8 tells of a widow who did not lose heart in prayer, and James tells us that "the prayer of a righteous man is powerful and effective" (James 5:16, NIV).

Take some time and memorize the Lord's Prayer. It may take you a few days or even a couple of weeks, but keep working at it. As you go through the Lord's Prayer, reflect on what each line means for you personally. Don't let this prayer be a dead ritual. Let it be a living tradition that you pray from the heart.

1. Why is the Lord's Prayer one of the most popular prayers of the Bible? What makes it such a universal prayer?

2. How does God, being your heavenly Father, impact and influence your understanding of prayer?

3. God is an awesome God who is worthy of praise. An important aspect of the Lord's Prayer is praise and making God's name holy. How does praise influence your personal prayer life?

4. The Lord's Prayer begins with God, His name, His kingdom, and His will. The prayer reminds us that this world belongs to God. Why should we pray for God's kingdom and His will to come?

5. Forgiveness is an important part of prayer and a great blessing that is unique to the Christian faith. Why is it so important to ask for God's forgiveness? How does that become the example for us to forgive others?

6. If God is already sovereign, why should we ask for God's protection for our lives?

THE ROAD AHEAD

The Road goes ever on and on. Down from the door where it began. Now far ahead the Road has gone, and I must follow, if I can.

J. R. R. TOLKIEN

WE HAVE COME to the end of the road. True, we could explore many other doctrines, but that is not the purpose of this book. I set out to provide you with a map to the basic essentials of the Christian faith through the lenses of the Apostles' Creed, the Ten Commandments, and the Lord's Prayer. These standards of our faith have stood the test of time and have the power to speak to our postmodern world. They have been battle tested and found to be true and essential in every generation. We need to keep the past and the future in perpetual conversation so we can have a fresh expression of the timeless gospel in the twenty-first century.

In conclusion, the Apostles' Creed, the Ten Commandments, and the Lord's Prayer have helped me in several important and surprising ways. First, they helped me realize that I am a part of the larger Christian family whose roots go back to the time of Christ. Too often, contemporary Christians forget that there have been two thousand years of church history—full of amazing stories of great men and women who helped change the course of history and fought to pass on the faith so future generations may believe. We are indebted to them. It is not too much to say that we are here today because of their faith.

For years I felt like a spiritual orphan who was unaware of having a rich family heritage and roots. Then, like someone who discovered his family genealogy for the first time, I discovered my spiritual family tree. Robert Webber reminds us,

> Our family tree begins not with the Reformation or the twentieth-century evangelical movement but with Jesus Christ, and it continues through the Apostles, the primitive Christian community, the Apostolic Fathers, the Eastern Orthodox Church, the Catholic Church, the Church of the Reformation, and all who say, "Jesus is Lord."[1]

Secondly, these doctrines help me live out my Christian faith. I'd be lost without them. Let me explain: They provide a moral and doctrinal compass for Christians. They help us navigate our way around the larger story of God. Like a road map, they provide us with a clear and concise summary of what Christians should know and believe from the Bible. Theologian and author J. I. Packer says, "The hundred-word Apostles' Creed is the simplified road map, ignoring much but enabling you to see at a glance the main points of Christian belief."[2]

Christian doctrine is not just for knowing, but for living. The essentials give us a foundation to build our life upon. What we believe about God, Jesus, and the Holy Spirit shapes and influences how we live and how we see the rest of the world:

- God is the Creator of all things, so I should care for His creation.
- Jesus died for my sin, so I must live for Him and share my faith with others.
- God created us to live in community, so I need the church.

In the end, a creed is not just what we believe but how we live out what we believe.

I hope I have sparked a hunger and curiosity in you to learn more about the historic Christian faith. It doesn't end here. You can go as deep as you want to go. I have recommended a list of books on various issues and topics (see pages 131–133) that will help you explore other areas that are relevant to your faith. There are many other historic creeds, confessions, and catechisms. You can learn more about them as well as find additional ways to connect to the essentials of historic Christian faith at www.creedthebook.com.

NICENE AND ATHANASIAN CREEDS

NICENE CREED

We believe in one God,
the Father almighty,
maker of heaven and earth,
of all things visible and invisible.

And in one Lord Jesus Christ,
the only Son of God,
begotten from the Father before all ages,
God from God,
Light from Light,
true God from true God,
begotten, not made;
of the same essence as the Father.
Through him all things were made.
For us and for our salvation
he came down from heaven;
he became incarnate by the Holy Spirit and the virgin Mary,
and was made human.
He was crucified for us under Pontius Pilate;
he suffered and was buried.
The third day he rose again, according to the Scriptures.

He ascended to heaven
and is seated at the right hand of the Father.
He will come again with glory
to judge the living and the dead.
His kingdom will never end.

And we believe in the Holy Spirit,
the Lord, the giver of life.
He proceeds from the Father and the Son,
and with the Father and the Son is worshiped and glorified.
He spoke through the prophets.
We believe in one holy catholic and apostolic church.
We affirm one baptism for the forgiveness of sins.
We look forward to the resurrection of the dead,
and to life in the world to come. Amen.[1]

ATHANASIAN CREED

Whoever desires to be saved should above all hold to the catholic faith.

Anyone who does not keep it whole and unbroken will doubtless perish
    eternally.

Now this is the catholic faith:

That we worship one God in trinity and the trinity in unity,
neither blending their persons
nor dividing their essence.
For the person of the Father is a distinct person,
the person of the Son is another,
and that of the Holy Spirit still another.
But the divinity of the Father, Son, and Holy Spirit is one,
their glory equal, their majesty coeternal.

What quality the Father has, the Son has, and the Holy Spirit has.
The Father is uncreated,

the Son is uncreated,
the Holy Spirit is uncreated.

The Father is immeasurable,
the Son is immeasurable,
the Holy Spirit is immeasurable.

The Father is eternal,
the Son is eternal,
the Holy Spirit is eternal.

And yet there are not three eternal beings;
there is but one eternal being.
So too there are not three uncreated or immeasurable beings;
there is but one uncreated and immeasurable being.

Similarly, the Father is almighty,
the Son is almighty,
the Holy Spirit is almighty.
Yet there are not three almighty beings;
there is but one almighty being.

Thus the Father is God,
the Son is God,
the Holy Spirit is God.
Yet there are not three gods;
there is but one God.

Thus the Father is Lord,
the Son is Lord,
the Holy Spirit is Lord.
Yet there are not three lords;
there is but one Lord.

Just as Christian truth compels us
to confess each person individually
as both God and Lord,

so catholic religion forbids us
to say that there are three gods or lords.

The Father was neither made nor created nor begotten from anyone.
The Son was neither made nor created;
he was begotten from the Father alone.
The Holy Spirit was neither made nor created nor begotten;
he proceeds from the Father and the Son.

Accordingly there is one Father, not three fathers;
there is one Son, not three sons;
there is one Holy Spirit, not three holy spirits.

Nothing in this trinity is before or after,
nothing is greater or smaller;
in their entirety the three persons
are coeternal and coequal with each other.

So in everything, as was said earlier,
we must worship their trinity in their unity
and their unity in their trinity.

Anyone then who desires to be saved
should think thus about the trinity.

But it is necessary for eternal salvation
that one also believe in the incarnation
of our Lord Jesus Christ faithfully.

Now this is the true faith:

That we believe and confess
that our Lord Jesus Christ, God's Son,
is both God and human, equally.

He is God from the essence of the Father,
begotten before time;
and he is human from the essence of his mother,

born in time;
completely God, completely human,
with a rational soul and human flesh;
equal to the Father as regards divinity,
less than the Father as regards humanity.

Although he is God and human,
yet Christ is not two, but one.
He is one, however,
not by his divinity being turned into flesh,
but by God's taking humanity to himself.
He is one,
certainly not by the blending of his essence,
but by the unity of his person.
For just as one human is both rational soul and flesh,
so too the one Christ is both God and human.

He suffered for our salvation;
he descended to hell;
he arose from the dead;
he ascended to heaven;
he is seated at the Father's right hand;
from there he will come to judge the living and the dead.
At his coming all people will arise bodily
and give an accounting of their own deeds.
Those who have done good will enter eternal life,
and those who have done evil will enter eternal fire.

This is the catholic faith:
one cannot be saved without believing it firmly and faithfully.[2]

READING LIST

HERE IS A list of books that you may find helpful as you grow deeper in your faith. It's by no means exhaustive; rather, these are a few books that I have found helpful along my personal journey. Enjoy.

BASIC CHRISTIAN BELIEFS

Basic Christianity by John Stott
Christian Beliefs: Twenty Basics Every Christian Should Know by Wayne Grudem
The Christian Life: A Doctrinal Introduction by Sinclair Ferguson
Concise Theology by J. I. Packer
Know What You Believe by Paul E. Little
Knowing God by J. I. Packer
The Knowledge of the Holy by A. W. Tozer
Mere Christianity by C. S. Lewis

CHURCH HISTORY

Church History in Plain Language by Bruce L. Shelley
Historical Theology: An Introduction to the History of Christian Thought by Alister E. McGrath
The Story of Christian Theology: Twenty Centuries of Tradition and Reform by Roger E. Olson
Turning Points: Decisive Moments in the History of Christianity by Mark A. Noll

FAITH AND CULTURE

Christ and Culture by H. Richard Niebuhr

Counterfeit Gods: The Empty Promises of Money, Sex, and Power, and the Only Hope That Matters by Timothy Keller

Culture Making: Recovering Our Creative Calling by Andy Crouch

The Radical Reformission: Reaching Out Without Selling Out by Mark Driscoll

The Reason for God: Belief in an Age of Skepticism by Timothy Keller

INTRODUCTION TO CREEDS AND CATECHISMS

The Big Book of Questions and Answers: A Family Devotional Guide to the Christian Faith by Sinclair B. Ferguson

Big Truths for Young Hearts: Teaching and Learning the Greatness of God by Bruce A. Ware

The Good News We Almost Forgot: Rediscovering the Gospel in a 16th Century Catechism by Kevin DeYoung

Rediscovering Catechism: The Art of Equipping Covenant Children by Donald Van Dyken

Training Hearts, Teaching Minds: Family Devotions Based on the Shorter Catechism by Starr Meade

SPIRITUAL GROWTH

A Long Obedience in the Same Direction: Discipleship in an Instant Society by Eugene H. Peterson

The Call: Finding and Fulfilling the Central Purpose of Your Life by Os Guiness

Celebration of Discipline: The Path to Spiritual Growth by Richard J. Foster

Confessions by Augustine

Desiring God: Meditations of a Christian Hedonist by John Piper

The Discipline of Grace: God's Role and Our Role in the Pursuit of Holiness by Jerry Bridges

The Gospel for Real Life: Turn to the Liberating Power of the Cross . . . Every Day by Jerry Bridges

The Pilgrim's Progress by John Bunyan

The Walk: Steps for New and Renewed Followers of Jesus by Stephen Smallman

STUDYING THE BIBLE

How to Read the Bible for All Its Worth by Gordon D. Fee and Douglas Stuart

Interpreting the Synoptic Gospels (Guides to New Testament Exegesis) by Scot McKnight

New Testament Documents: Are They Reliable? by F. F. Bruce

Scriptures and Truth by D. A. Carson and John D. Woodbridge

Survey of the Bible by William Hendriksen

NOTES

Introduction

1. C. S. Lewis, *Mere Christianity* (New York: Collier Books, 1952), vi.
2. G. K. Chesterton, *Orthodoxy* (New York: Barnes & Noble, 2007), 5.

Part 1: The Apostles' Creed

1. This line in the Creed is somewhat controversial. There are several different ideas to what exactly this means. It is important to note that the line "he descended to hell" doesn't appear anywhere in the Bible. Many scholars agree this simply meant that He actually experienced a "state of death" in the grave until His resurrection. The Westminster Larger Catechism, Question 50 says, "Christ's humiliation after his death consisted in his being buried, and continuing in the state of the dead, and under the power of death till the third day; which has been otherwise expressed in these words, he descended into hell."
2. The word *catholic* means "universal."
3. Apostles' Creed, from the Christian Reformed Church, http://www.crcna.org/pages/apostles_creed.cfm.

Chapter 1: I Believe

1. See "Most American Christians Do Not Believe That Satan or the Holy Spirit Exist," http://www.barna.org/barna-update/article/12-faithspirituality/260-most-american-christians-do-not-believe-that-satan-or-the-holy-spirit-exist.
2. Sally Lloyd-Jones, *The Jesus Storybook Bible* (Grand Rapids, MI: Zondervan, 2007), 17.
3. Jerry Bridges, *The Discipline of Grace: God's Role and Our Role in the Pursuit of Holiness* (Colorado Springs, CO: NavPress, 1973), 22.
4. A. W. Tozer, *The Pursuit of God* (Camp Hill, PA: Christian Publications, 1993), 9.

Chapter 2: God

1. Alvin L. Reid, *Radically Unchurched: Who They Are and How to Reach Them* (Grand Rapids, MI: Kregel, 2002), 21.
2. John Owen, *Communion with God: Fellowship with Father, Son and Holy Spirit* (Carlisle, PA: Banner of Truth, 2000), 27.
3. J. I. Packer, *Knowing God* (Downers Grove, IL: InterVarsity, 1993), 86.
4. J. I. Packer discusses God's omniscience in *Concise Theology—A Guide to Historic Christian Beliefs* (Wheaton, IL: Tyndale, 1993), 31–32. *Omniscient* is a word that means "knowing everything." Scripture declares that God's eyes run everywhere (see Job 24:23; Psalm 33:13-15; 139:13-16; Proverbs 15:3; Jeremiah 16:17; Hebrews 4:13). He searches all hearts and observes everyone's ways (see 1 Samuel 16:7; 1 Kings 8:39; 1 Chronicles 28:9; Psalm 139:1-6,23; Jeremiah 17:10; Luke 16:15; Romans 8:27; Revelation 2:23). In other words, God knows everything about everything and everybody all the time. He knows the future as well as the past and the present, and also about possible events that never happen (see 1 Samuel 23:9-13; 2 Kings 13:19; Psalm 81:14-15; Isaiah 48:18). All God's knowledge is always immediately and directly before His mind; He does not "access" information about things, as a computer might retrieve a file. Bible writers stand in awe of the capacity of God's mind in this regard (see Psalm 139:1-6; 147:5; Isaiah 40:13-14,28; cf. Romans 11:33-36).
5. Packer, *Concise Theology*, 35–36.
6. Quoted in John Piper, *Let the Nations Be Glad! The Supremacy of God in Missions* (Grand Rapids, MI: Baker, 1993), 12.
7. Learn more about Evangelical Environmental Network at www.creationcare .org. EEN was founded in 1993, and its work is grounded in the Bible's teaching on the responsibility of God's people to "tend the garden" and in a desire to be faithful to Jesus Christ and to follow Him. EEN publishes materials to equip and inspire individuals, families, and churches. It seeks to educate and mobilize people to make a difference in their churches and communities and to speak out on national and international policies that affect our ability to preach the gospel, protect life, and care for God's creation.
8. George G. Hunter III, *The Celtic Way of Evangelism: How Christianity Can Reach the West . . . Again* (Nashville: Abingdon, 2000), 50–51.

Chapter 3: Jesus Christ

1. Mark Driscoll and Gerry Breshears, *Vintage Jesus* (Wheaton, IL: Crossway, 2007), 15.

2. As a man, Jesus was born of a woman (see Luke 2:7). He grew up (see Luke 2:40,52). He got tired (see John 4:6). He got thirsty (see John 19:28). He got hungry (see Matthew 4:2). He became physically weak (see Matthew 4:11; Luke 23:26). He died (see Luke 23:46). And He had a real human body after His resurrection (see Luke 24:39; John 20:20,27).

3. Jesus claimed to do only things that God could do (see John 8:28-29). He claimed to be sinless (see John 8:46-47). He said He is the only way to God (see John 14:6; Matthew 11:27). He claimed to be able to forgive sins (see Luke 5:20-21; 7:48-49). He said He would die and come back to life (see John 10:17; 12:32-33; 16:16; Luke 18:31-33). He promised everlasting life (see John 6:40,47; 10:28-30; 11:25). He accepted worship (see Matthew 8:2; 14:33; 28:9,17; John 9:38).

4. Robert Coleman, *The Master Plan of Evangelism* (Grand Rapids, MI: Revell, 1993), 27.

5. See the Gospels for the suffering that Jesus endured: Matthew 26–27; Mark 15; Luke 22–23; John 18–19.

6. "Because He Lives," words and music by William J. Gaither, © 1971 BMI.

7. Malcolm McDow and Alvin L. Reid, *Firefall: How God Has Shaped History Through Revivals* (Nashville: Broadman & Holman, 1997), 94.

8. Thomas Jackson, ed., *The Works of John Wesley* (Grand Rapids, MI: Baker, 1979), 1:103.

9. Dietrich Bonhoeffer, *The Cost of Discipleship* (New York: Touchstone, 1995), 89.

10. C. S. Lewis, *Mere Christianity* (New York: Collier Books, 1952), 72.

Chapter 4: The Holy Spirit

1. The Holy Spirit is omnipresent (see Psalm 139:7-10); omnipotent (see Luke 1:35); omniscient (see 1 Corinthians 2:10-11); eternal (see Hebrews 9:14); holy (see Matthew 12:31). The titles given to the Holy Spirit also reveal His divine nature: "Spirit of Christ" (1 Peter 1:11); "Spirit of God" (Genesis 1:2; Job 33:4; Romans 8:11); "Spirit of glory" (1 Peter 4:14); "Spirit of the Lord" (Isaiah 61:1); "Spirit of the Father" (Matthew 10:20); Spirit of the Son (see Galatians 4:6); "power of the Highest" (Luke 1:35, NKJV); "Spirit of holiness" (Romans 1:4); "Spirit of knowledge" (Isaiah 11:2); "Spirit of life" (Romans 8:2; see also Revelation 11:11); "Spirit of . . . might" (Isaiah 11:2); "eternal Spirit" (Hebrews 9:14); "Spirit of truth" (John 14:17; 15:26).

2. Nicene Creed, from the Christian Reformed Church, http://www.crcna.org/pages/nicene_creed.cfm. Find the complete Nicene Creed in the appendix (on page 125).

3. The personal nature of the Holy Spirit: The Holy Spirit can be lied to (see Acts 5:3); grieved (see Ephesians 4:30); quenched (see 1 Thessalonians 5:19); resisted (see Acts 7:51); and blasphemed (see Matthew 12:31-32; Mark 3:28-29; Luke 12:10).

4. John Owen, *Communion with God* (Carlisle, PA: Banner of Truth, 1991), 168.

5. Wayne Grudem and Stanley N. Gundry, eds., *Are Miracles for Today?* (Grand Rapids, MI: Zondervan, 1996). This book offers a more in-depth discussion on the different views of spiritual gifts.

6. Wayne Grudem, *Systematic Theology* (Grand Rapids, MI: Zondervan, 1994), 1016.

7. Owen, 97.

8. A few examples are Nathan and David in the Old Testament (see 2 Samuel 12:1-14) and Agabus and Paul in the New Testament (see Acts 21:10-11).

9. David Martyn Lloyd-Jones, *The Sovereign Spirit* (Wheaton, IL: Harold Shaw Publishers, 1985), 48.

10. Lloyd-Jones, 48.

Chapter 5: The Church

1. The National Council of Churches recently released its annual yearbook, *2008 Yearbook of American & Canadian Churches*. Among the top twenty-five churches, only five reported membership increases. All other communions in the top twenty-five said they lost members or reported no increases or decreases.

2. David T. Olson, *The American Church in Crisis* (Grand Rapids, MI: Zondervan, 2008), 29.

3. Tim Stafford, "The Church—Why Bother?" *Christianity Today*, 49, no. 1 (January 2005): 42–49.

4. Gene A. Getz, *The Measure of a Church* (Ventura, CA: Regal, 2001), 18.

5. John Stott, "The Living God Is a Missionary God," quoted in James E. Berney, ed., *You Can Tell the World* (Downer Grove, IL: InterVarsity, 1979), 9.

6. C. S. Lewis, *God in the Dock: Essays on Theology and Ethics* (Grand Rapids, MI: Eerdmans, 1970), 91–92.

7. Stephen Smallman, *The Walk: Steps for New and Renewed Followers of Jesus* (Phillipsburg, NJ: P&R, 2010), 186.

8. See Matthew 26:26-27; Mark 14:22-23; Luke 22:17-19; 1 Corinthians 11:20-24.

9. John S. Hammett, *Biblical Foundations for Baptist Churches: A Contemporary Ecclesiology* (Grand Rapids, MI: Kregel, 2005), 278.

10. Albert Outler, *John Wesley* (New York: Oxford University Press, 2008), 336.
11. John Calvin, *Institutes of the Christian Religion* (Philadelphia: Westminster, 1996), 21:1025–1026 (4.1.9).
12. Mark Liederbach and Alvin L. Reid, *The Convergent Church: Missional Worshipers in an Emerging Culture* (Grand Rapids, MI: Kregel, 2009), 145.
13. Mark Dever, *Nine Marks of a Healthy Church* (Wheaton, IL: Crossway, 2004), 16.
14. Martin Luther, *Table Talk* (New York: Dover, 2005), 35.
15. See National Center on Family Homelessness at http://www.familyhomelessness.org/facts.php?p=sm.

Chapter 6: Forgiveness and Eternal Life

1. Philip Yancey, *What's So Amazing About Grace?* (Grand Rapids, MI: Zondervan, 1997), 45.
2. Jerry Bridges, *Transforming Grace: Living Confidently in God's Unfailing Love* (Colorado Springs, CO: NavPress, 1991), 21–22.
3. Charles Spurgeon, *C. H. Spurgeon Autobiography: Volume 1, The Early Years* (Carlisle, PA: Banner of Truth, 1962), 164–165.
4. Roland H. Bainton, *Here I Stand: A Life of Martin Luther* (Peabody, MA: Hendrickson Publishers, 1977), 48.
5. Don Carson, *Cross and Christian Ministry: Leadership Lessons from 1 Corinthians* (Grand Rapids, MI: Baker, 1993), 26.
6. See the Cambridge Declaration at Alliance of Confessing Evangelicals wesite, http://www.alliancenet.org/partner/Article_Display_Page/0,,PTID307086_CHID798774_CIID1411364,00.html.
7. Stephen E. Smallman, *Spiritual Birthline: Understanding How We Experience the New Birth* (Wheaton, IL: Crossway, 2006), 24.
8. Donald S. Whitney, *Spiritual Disciplines for the Christian Life* (Colorado Springs, CO: NavPress, 1991).
9. Wayne Grudem, *Systematic Theology* (Grand Rapids, MI: Zondervan, 2000).

Chapter 7: Whatever Happened to Morality?

1. See Barna Group, http://www.barna.org.
2. John Calvin, *The Golden Booklet of the True Christian Life* (Grand Rapids, MI: Baker, 1952), 11–13.
3. Timothy Keller, *Counterfeit Gods: The Empty Promises of Money, Sex, and Power, and the Only Hope That Matters* (New York: Dutton, 2009).
4. See Matthew 15:4; 19:19; Mark 7:10; 10:19; Luke 18:20; Ephesians 6:2-4.

5. God placed a high standard on the Jewish family and expected the Israelite children to respect and honor their parents because the family brought stability to the ancient Israelite society. This commandment came with a promised blessing and a reminder of the importance of the family as an honored institution. Disobedience to this command resulted in capital punishment (see Deuteronomy 21:18-21). One of the reasons for the Babylonian captivity was due to the lack of honoring parents (see Ezekiel 22:7,15).
6. See Proverbs 13:24; Ephesians 6:4; Hebrews 12:5-11.
7. Quote taken from *The Lord of the Rings: The Fellowship of the Ring*, New Line Cinema, an AOL Time Warner Company, 2001.

Chapter 8: Learning to Pray Like Jesus

1. Andrew Murray, *With Christ in the School of Prayer* (Westwood, NJ: Barbour, 1986), 25–26.
2. See Ephesians 1:15-23; 3:14-20.

Conclusion

1. Robert Webber, *Evangelicals on the Canterbury Trail: Why Evangelicals Are Attracted to the Liturgical Church* (Harrisburg, PA: Morehouse, 1985), 64.
2. J. I. Packer, *Affirming the Apostles' Creed* (Wheaton, IL: Crossway, 2008), 11.

Appendix

1. Nicene Creed, from the Christian Reformed Church, http://www.crcna.org/pages/nicene_creed.cfm.
2. Athanasian Creed, from the Christian Reformed Church, http://www.crcna.org/pages/athanasian_creed.cfm.

ABOUT THE AUTHOR

WINFIELD BEVINS serves as lead pastor of Church of the Outer Banks, which he founded in 2005. His life's passion in ministry is discipleship and helping start new churches. Winfield speaks at conferences and retreats throughout the United States on a variety of topics. He is the author of dozens of articles as well as several popular e-books, including *Grow: Reproducing Through Organic Discipleship.* He has a doctorate from Southeastern Baptist Theological Seminary in Wake Forest, North Carolina. Winfield, his wife, Kay, and their two daughters live in the outer banks, where he loves to surf and spend time at the beach with his family and friends.

WAIT... THERE'S MORE!

FREE ONLINE TOOLS
for churches and small groups

CreedTheBook.com

Visit **CreedTheBook.com** to engage with Winfield Bevins on the ideas in the book and to find additional resources that will help you and your church connect to the essentials of historic Christian faith. On this site, you will find practical information on how to use the study as a churchwide discipleship strategy. Other free downloads include a small-group leader's guide and sermon outlines.

CreedTheBook.com

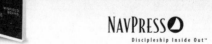